TWENTIETH CENTURY VIEWS

The aim of this series is to present the best
in contemporary critical opinion on major
authors, providing a twentieth century perspective on their changing status in an era
of profound revaluation.

Maynard Mack, *Series Editor*
Yale University

GIDE

A COLLECTION OF CRITICAL ESSAYS

Edited by
David Littlejohn

Prentice-Hall, Inc. *Englewood Cliffs, N. J.*
A SPECTRUM BOOK

To Jean Hytier and Albert Guerard

Contents

GIDE

Introduction

by David Littlejohn

I

The story of Gide's relations with his critics is dramatic and revealing, as such stories go. The reader of his *Journal* will note the frequency and intensity with which he does battle with his critics, for thirty years protesting their refusal to notice him, then for another thirty years attacking their misinterpretations of his purposes or his work.

Before 1920 almost none of Gide's works sold more than a few hundred copies (he was forced to pay the printing costs of his first twenty-three books) or received even a passing glance from influential critics. The best he could usually hope for was a review from some friend like Francis Jammes or Henri Ghéon and the usually disdainful notice of the *Mercure de France*. A sympathetic essay on *La Porte étroite* (*Strait Is the Gate*) by the English critic Edmund Gosse in 1909 was an occasion for great joy. The leading Paris critic, Paul Souday, did deign to notice that work and it achieved what was for Gide a considerable success—an edition of 1,000 copies was sold out within a week.

Writing two years later in *Le Temps* (the predecessor of today's *Le Monde*), Souday was to blame Gide for much of his own critical neglect. After the dismal failures of his first books, Gide had adopted the face-saving strategy of printing very small editions, refusing to curry favors or even to send out review copies, and of appearing thereby to invite the silence he knew he was going to get anyway. But there can be no question that he was wounded by the inattention. "I am beginning to be tired of *not being*. . . . Wounded vanity has never produced anything that matters, but at times my pride suffers from a real despair. And I live certain days as if in the nightmare of the man who was walled up alive in his tomb . . ." (*Journal*, 1907).

By the end of the 1920s most of Gide's books were back in print. *Les Nourritures terrestres (Fruits of the Earth)* had become a *cause célèbre* and was selling in the tens of thousands. The first English translations of his novels began appearing in 1920 and by 1927, with the appearance of *The Counterfeiters (Les Faux-Monnayeurs)*, he was being ranked by popular American reviewers as the peer of Proust, Joyce, and Mann. Now every serious review was commenting on his books as they came off the press; few important French writers of the twenties and thirties failed to comment on the Gide phenomenon; and outside of France his work was accorded the attention due that of an international master. He was the subject of panel discussions, public opinion polls, and special issues of magazines; every analysis of the "New Novel" had to find room for *Les Faux-Monnayeurs*.

Can we identify the moment of Gide's emergence into the light? Most of those who have tried to plot the curve of his reputation have pointed to the public notice paid to him by three men, in 1921, 1922, and 1923. The first was Henri Massis, a spokesman for traditional France, who accurately saw, and vividly denounced, the danger Gide's "immoralism," his concept of a self-determined ethic, represented to traditional values. "What he is questioning is the very notion of *man* on which we live." The second was Henri Béraud, a petty journalist who undertook a campaign against what he regarded as the exaggerated and "un-French" influence of Gide and his colleagues at the *Nouvelle Revue Française*—a campaign which had no effect other than to make its subjects far better known than they had been before. "These attacks have made me more famous in three months than my books had done in thirty years," Gide wrote to his *Journal*. The third was Roger Martin du Gard, a close friend who cited Gide's 26-year-old *Les Nourritures terrestres* in the 1923 installment of his own best-selling novel, *Les Thibault*, dramatizing it as a decisive influence in the life of one of his fictional characters.

> The whole afternoon went to its perusal, and he read it [*Les Nourritures terrestres*] at one sitting. He left the house at nightfall. Never had his mind been in such ferment, uplifted by such splendid visions. He walked on and on, taking long strides—a conqueror's progress. Night came on. He had been following the bank of the Seine and was very far from home. He dined off a roll and returned; the book lay on his table, awaiting him. Should he, or should he not . . . ? Daniel dared not open it again. Finally he went to bed, but did not sleep. At last he capitulated and, wrapping a dressing-gown around

him, slowly read the book once more, from beginning to end. He knew well that this was a momentous hour for him, that at the deepest levels of his consciousness a slow, mysterious process of gestation was at work. When with the dawn he turned, for the second time, the final page, he found that he now looked on life with new eyes.

In the next few years thousands of young men, discovering this little "manual of liberation" for the first time, seem to have undergone something like the experience of Daniel de Fontanin.

But Massis, Béraud, and Martin du Gard are only the proximate occasions of Gide's arrival at center stage. The crucial public event in Gide's career was the war that had ended several years earlier. The undreamed-of horrors of the First World War convinced many people of the bankruptcy of those very traditional "notions of man" Gide had been censured for questioning. The experience of war brought many Europeans—especially young Europeans—to something very like the state of stark, unsupported moral self-dependence Gide had chosen for himself years before. In attacking André Gide, Henri Massis was really lamenting the proud, even defiant, to him wicked independence of God declared by much of the Western world after 1918. This is not to deny the "influence" so often attributed to Gide or his role in fostering this independence; only to insist that there were other and more powerful reasons for it than the willing scapegoat Massis had chosen.

Once he had been lifted into celebrity by the postwar mood and certain postwar publicists, almost everything Gide did during the next fifteen years served to maintain and enlarge his notoriety. If he was partly responsible for his own years of critical neglect, he was also certainly a skillful promoter of his subsequent fame. *Corydon* in 1924, *Si le grain ne meurt* (*If It Die*) and *Les Faux-Monnayeurs* in 1926 were regarded by many right-thinking men as a concerted trilogy of public outrage, a shameless confession and defense of the most unspeakable practices. By attacking the French colonial system in his *Voyage au Congo* (*Travels in the Congo*) of 1927, Gide provoked another round of abuse and defense.

Gide's political activity in the 1930s, if not his literary work, guaranteed him a continuance of notoriety. The controversy over his profession of faith in the Soviet Union (1932) was exceeded only by that over his anti-Stalinist *Retour de l'U.R.S.S.* (*Return from the U.S.S.R.*) in 1936, which gained him more press space—in America as well as Europe—than he had obtained during any other year of his life. Nor did his fame end with the thirties, despite a considerable recession in his reputation at the time of the war. In 1947 he received the Nobel Prize for Literature and the renewed attention of the literary world. His death in 1951 provoked tidal waves of tribute and attack, the latter cresting the following year when his entire work was condemned to the Roman Catholic Index of Forbidden Books —a dubious tribute he shares with a great number of the leading figures in French literature.

II

This collection of critical essays in no way pretends to represent Gide's reputation or reception over the last eighty years. I did not intend it to be a little museum of changing critical tastes, but rather sought for the best and most useful shorter secondary sources for the present day student of Gide: a selection of works that would cover as many as possible of the essential aspects of the case of André Gide (the *Journal,* the most important works, the sexual, religious, and political questions, his ethic, his style, his moral and literary influence, his continuing relevance, his moral worth as a man), and at the same time compose itself into some kind of balanced statement, all within the compact limits of this series.

I found nothing worthy of inclusion written earlier than 1938. The earliest piece here is a selection from a still-unsurpassed study written by Jean Hytier in Gide's sixty-ninth year. What is surprising, though, is not that it took Gide so long to receive intelligent critical attention, but that Professor Hytier was able to penetrate the fog of controversy and misapprehension as early as 1938. In 1938, as in every year since Gide first emerged out of the coteries in the early 1920s, it was almost impossible for readers or critics to see him except in terms of various distorting popular images. Very few of the hundreds of articles and books[1] written during the period of Gide's greatest fame could be of service today to anyone, except the cultural antiquarian, the chronicler of long-forgotten literary battles.

I considered including, and in a longer anthology would have included, only one essay earlier than Professor Hytier's—the first half of Jacques Rivière's very lyrical, soulful *étude* of 1911, a kind

---

[1] Pierre Lafille lists 657 works on Gide, including 38 books, published in France between 1920 and 1939, in his unpublished thesis, "André Gide et l'opinion en France de 1890 à 1950"; and this is only a sampling of the more important, generally Parisian sources.

of psycho-musical analysis of Gide's style by one of his earliest and most sensitive disciples, much of which still seems moving and true. The reader of French may still benefit from the prewar studies of François-Paul Alibert, Claude-Louis Estève, and particularly Ramon Fernandez (see Bibliography); and Professor Hytier's whole book remains essential. But for the most part, Gide had to wait until after World War II for the tribute of clear-headed critical insight.

Some of the reasons for this long wait for the appearance of sensitive and acute criticism have already been mentioned. They include Gide's own hostility to and pretended disdain for most criticism; his willful frustrating of critics and readers; the bewildering problems presented by his "image" and his "influence" that arose almost at once when he finally arrived on the public scene, in great part as a result of the moral and political scandals he seemed determined to arouse. He often claimed himself to be writing, like Stendhal, not for his own generation but for generations to come, and took what comfort he could in identifying himself with neglected masters of the past, like Keats and Baudelaire: "I think of Keats. I tell myself that two or three passionate admirations like mine would have kept him alive. Useless efforts. I feel at times utterly enervated by the silence" (*Journal*, 1907).

The two world wars, as we have seen, served as watersheds in the terrain of Gide's reputation. The first allowed a generation of Frenchmen to grow up to, to come suddenly to need the support of his private insights of ten or twenty years before. Out of this need were born testimonials like Daniel de Fontanin's; out of the service (or disservice) he and his works performed in the twenties and thirties grew scandal, polemic, notoriety, and defense. But it was scarcely the proper climate for reasoned evaluations.

With the second war came new needs and new values; the decline of interest in Gide and his writings between 1936–37 (the year of the *Retour de l'U.R.S.S.* scandal) and 1939 is decidedly abrupt. He had suddenly lost all that furious contemporaneity; alongside Sartre, Malraux, and Camus he seemed very old, almost irrelevant. But what was gone was only a need that had sustained a false, or at least partial, image of Gide; he and his works were still there, waiting for intelligent attention.

Nor had they long to wait. The six years' buffer zone of war and, on Gide's part, of virtual silence, was precisely what was needed. That distance traversed, the cooler assessments—in effect, almost the first genuinely useful assessments—could begin.

Two of the earliest—Gaëtan Picon's still-valid defense of 1946 and Maurice Blanchot's brilliant analysis of 1947 (perhaps the finest essay ever written on Gide)—are included here. It may seem foolish to identify a time so recent as a concluded critical "period," but the record would appear to distinguish the decade that followed these essays (1946–56) as the "golden age," by far the most thoughtful and fruitful decade in the history of Gide criticism. From these ten years, five years on either side of Gide's death in 1951, years which englobe the publication of the *Journal* in English, the condemnation of Rome, a nine-page profile in *Time*, and a Nobel Prize for Literature —from these years came the serious studies by Roger Bastide, Etiemble, Jacques Lévy (written earlier but published in 1954), Claude-Edmonde Magny, and Kurt Weinberg—any one of which another editor might have included here; the valuable *hommage* numbers of the *N.R.F.* and *Yale French Studies* in 1951; Pierre Lafille's Sorbonne thesis of 1953; the still-basic biographical works by Roger Martin du Gard, Jean Schlumberger, Claude Mauriac, and above all Jean Delay; the book-length critiques by Albert Guerard, Germaine Brée, Justin O'Brien, and Enid Starkie; as well as innumerable testimonials from the world of letters on the occasions of the Nobel Prize in 1947 and Gide's death in 1951.

It is from this decade, therefore, that the greater part of my selections were made. Serious work has been done since 1956, of course, much of it in the scholarly or "dissertation" vein represented here by Professor Knecht's essay on *La Porte étroite*. There were at least nine French theses and eight American or English dissertations on Gide under way at the start of 1970; four of these disciplined and limited studies have been published in the United States alone since 1967. It is difficult, however, to assert anything about Gide's present place or reputation from works such as these: they may represent no more than one safely "classical" author's share of the burgeoning graduate school population. The centennial year of 1969 brought exhibitions, television shows, colloquia, special issues of magazines, a "Chemin André Gide" in Uzès, and a green postage stamp bearing his likeness. But more impressive celebratory rituals were afforded Paul Claudel on his centennial the year before, and one wonders how long this ceremonial attention will last. There remains a great deal of work for the dedicated scholar—the editing of letters and texts, the biography beyond 1895—but it seems unlikely that the great flowering of critical insight of the ten years after the war will be equalled soon.

III

What is it that the best critics have to tell us of André Gide? The way to find out, obviously, is to read them, beginning, perhaps, with the samples here. But one may identify a few recurring themes.

One point emphasized by both friends and enemies is Gide's doing without God, his very consciously and willfully living his life and making his work with no reference to or dependence on other-worldly support. For critics like François Mauriac (and the anonymous commentator of *L'Osservatore Romano*), men for whom God does still rule the world, order it by laws and surround it by sanctions, Gide's example is at best pitiable, at worst heinous, by any count wrong. But for others, like Sartre, who believe themselves to be living in a godless universe, Gide's example was of great value. For he provided them with a vivid, ardent, and minutely recorded demonstration of how to live, how to lead a morally responsible life in such a place. "Gide cherishes, in all cases, one single wish: that of presenting (as he says of Goethe) an exemplary image 'of what man can attain on his own, without any recourse to Grace.' . . . He has never for a moment stopped believing that the only life we have is the one we lead on this earth—and that it is quite sufficient" (Gaëtan Picon).

Gide's exemplary role is something noted by almost every observer. "His life's work . . . [is] an attitude, proposed for our observation: an example of a way of life . . ." (Picon). He seems—if not in his everyday life, at least in his "Life," in the shaped and edited record of that life—to have regarded individual human existence as a moral test, something to be built day by day, something by which one will be judged—even though there are no rules but one's own, no judges but oneself. Because of the absence, in his universe, of external moral sanctions or supports, the test will be arduous, the judgment never certain, and anything like victory or success finally impossible. The origins of this radical Gidean impulse—to lead the moral life, even if one is alone, in a moral desert—may lie in his puritan childhood, his family situation, his nervous or sexual disorders. But to the sympathetic critic, the origins of the impulse are of less importance than the usable image and example provided by the long life and life's work that was its result.[2]

[2] "It is customary in our epoch to seek a psychological cause for intellectual

What matters finally, then, is not the means he chose for his own particular test, nor the line drawn by his own career, nor (least of all) the position we find him in at the end. What matters is the instance, the illuminating and liberating instance: the idea, the possibility he demonstrates of a life lived and made on such terms. If we are willing to risk heaven and hell—or, to put it another way, to risk all, to make of our lives the supreme *expérience*[3]—then here is one of the richest available models. But it is for each man to find his own means, to draw his own line, achieve his own end. "What matters . . . [is] having sought, without respite or relaxation, to give proof, in the most personal ways, of an effort in which one realizes the best in oneself" (Alain Girard).

The means Gide chose was art, or more precisely literature, words used as well as one can possibly use them. Many of Gide's critics, including some of the most perceptive and sympathetic (Brée, Delay, Martin du Gard) have regarded his faith in and dedication to literature as excessive and somehow inhuman. "For him, life was subsidiary to literature" (Germaine Brée); and much of Gide's career would seem to bear out this judgment. The great conjugal crisis of 1918 (his wife, despairing of her husband's affection or fidelity, burned all of his letters to her) may seem on first view to have affected Gide primarily as a writer. It is the loss of the precious pages ("I had never written any so pathetic") that has wounded him, the disfiguring of his publishable image—and not the raw private anguish the gesture represented. Claude Mauriac describes the encounters between his father and Gide, each rushing off afterwards to his respective journal to record his version of the meeting—as if mere "real life" did not count, somehow, until turned into words.

Not for one minute of his day, not for one minute of his sleepless night is his mind ever at rest, does his brain ever stop churning out materials for his books. . . . A *man of letters* from morning to night. Even in his pleasures, even in his amours. . . . The most fleeting impression is instantly captured, translated into the Gidean style, condensed into a formula marked with his seal, ready to *serve*. The sole end of his life is the enrichment of his work. . . .
(Martin du Gard, *Notes sur André Gide*)

---

impulses; and I am not saying that this is wrong; but I am saying that it is wrong to try to invalidate thereby the intrinsic value of the thought" (*Journal*, 1918).

[3] The French word signifies both "experience" and "experiment (test, trial)."

But such a view, according to Maurice Blanchot, does too little justice to the essential interdependence in Gide's venture between his life and his art. It is not, M. Blanchot declares, a matter of displacing one by the other; but of Gide's using art—of using words—as the ground whereon and the means whereby his own trial takes place, his own life is (or is not) justified. He attributes to Gide's example "the obligation felt by contemporary literature to be *more* than literature, to be a vital experience, an instrument of discovery, a way for man to test himself and, by means of this test, to strive (in vain) to outreach his grasp." "Art . . . from the point of view of the artist, a novel from the point of view of the novelist . . . the very fact of writing from the point of view of the one who writes—these are . . . a vital and dangerous experiment in which one is risking his very self, putting himself to the test." Others may, of course, elect to follow Gide's example without using Gide's means: but his way was words. The million words of the published *Journal* (selected, Alain Girard implies, out of thousands more, the omitting, the editing being part of the game); the experiments of *Les Nourritures terrestres, Saül, Paludes,* and other early works in which an attitude is tested or a tendency exorcised by being driven to its extreme; the large questions posed but never answered by the best *récits* (*L'Immoraliste, La Porte étroite*), so frustrating to traditional critics in their open-endedness, their refusal to conclude; that ultimate *roman d'aventures, Les Faux-Monnayeurs* ("the only one of his novels which fully expresses him": Germaine Brée)—these are the tokens and the instruments of Gide's particular vital adventure, the means by which he met the challenge of his particular life. Had he played the game otherwise and not left this verbal record behind, we should not have had (for better or worse) the model of a way of life which so many regard as Gide's primary legacy.

Seen as M. Blanchot would have us see it, the relationship between Gide's life and his written art has about it nothing arbitrary or mannered. The patently autobiographical nature of much of his fiction is something deeper and more complex than mere narcissism or exhibitionism. Yet so intimate and so obvious is this relationship, so copiously available are the life records, that it is the very rare critic of Gide's fiction who does not begin (or end) his work by pointing out the correspondences between Gide's stories and the events of his own life—guided, as often as not, by Gide's own admissions. André Water and Emmanuèle, Michel and Marceline, Jérôme and Alissa, the pastor and Amélie—how many critics

have taken pains to point out the links between each of these
couples and André and Madeleine Gide? In his "new reading" of
La Porte étroite included here, in fact, Professor Knecht defends
his interpretation of a line in the story by instancing a parallel line
out of *Et nunc manet in te,* Gide's intimate memoir of his own married life.

This pointing of correspondences is very often performed as a
crude and tactless critical act, undertaken out of a wrong-headed (or
at least very limited) conception of art and the creative process, and
with a view, frequently, to displaying deficiencies in either Gide's
talent or his character. If a novel "ought" to be life-like illusion
and nothing else, if fictional characters must seem wholly independent, fully-rounded people (in Forster's sense)—the sort of people you would recognize if you met them on the street, as we used
to say of the Rostovs—then surely Gide betrays his incompetence,
as well as his indiscretion, by telling no more than his own story
over and over, under any number of transparent disguises. "Certain
people refuse to acknowledge that I am a novelist," he complained,
and he worried whether they might be right. "Certain people" included his closest and wisest literary friend, Roger Martin du Gard,
an intransigent Tolstoyan in matters of fiction; one of those critics,
as M. Blanchot describes them, "for whom the only true novelist
is the teller of tales and the creator of characters."

I must confess that no critics of this persuasion are represented
here; I cannot see that they have anything useful to tell us about
the fictions of André Gide. His novels and tales *are* of a very special
kind, but it strikes me as more sensible to try to understand what
they are than to attack them for not being something else. Judged
by or read according to Tolstoyan standards, Gide's fictions may
well seem either half-disguised autobiography or excessively lucid
critical parables: limpid, stylized, rarefied Gidean spaces in which
thematic personages wander and meet according to an obviously
contrived schedule, at some remove from reality. But applying the
standard of "realism" to Gide's works makes about as much sense
as applying it to the plays of Bertold Brecht. Gide's novels and tales
are intended—like all of his life and work—as conscious moral
tests: tests of his fictional characters and their ideas, of course, but
also of the novelist, and of us. And the means he chooses is the
experimental novel: experimental sometimes in form (*Les Faux-
Monnayeurs,* a novel whose structure questions the whole business

of fiction), but always in essence, even in his most classical compositions: the novel *as* experiment.

All this is admirably seen and explained by critics like Germaine Brée and Jean Hytier. Professor Hytier responds to the formal nature of Gide's work—to its structure, rhythm, tone, and narrative technique—like a master musician responding to a complex piece of music that he understands and loves. His explication of the subtle strategy of Gide's art, the means by which, the ends to which he entangles and implicates *us* in his and his characters' moral dilemmas, strikes me as absolutely just. Professor Brée's essay on the work Gide called his "only novel" is more traditional, less rigorously formal in approach. But she, like Hytier, is fully aware that novels are structures, forms, autonomous constructs, and not life; not even necessarily imitations of or attempts to create life; and that Gide's, in particular, are closed fictional worlds he contrives in order to display and to criticize characters trapped by restrictive moral formulas, by fixed and partial ideals.

Several of the critics here do point out life-to-art correspondences of the sort I have mentioned—most notably Loring D. Knecht and Albert Guerard—but always, or almost always, with a scrupulousness of method and a respect for the integrity of the created work, the complexity of the creative act that render their biographical conjectures all the more persuasive. One may quarrel with certain steps in, certain aspects of their readings; Professor Knecht's Jérôme-centered reading of *La Porte étroite,* for example, may be not so much exclusive of as coexistent with the more traditional, Alissa-centered reading. But I no longer find it possible to read the two works in question (*Le Voyage d'Urien* and *La Porte étroite*) without seeing in their depths at least a strong shadow of what these men have seen, and appreciating how much the right kind of psychological criticism can enlarge and illuminate a literary text. Professor Guerard discovers barely-transformed confessions of an almost manic auto-eroticism; Professor Knecht evidence of a fear of impotence, a fear of heterosexual union itself. And yet there is no scandal-mongering, nothing reductive or unliterary in either study. Gide's sexual life was an essential determinant of the nature of his art, since it was so essential a part of the private moral battle he was fighting by means of his art; it is something impossible to ignore. But it is more than possible to misconstrue it, or to distort its role: it is so easy that almost everyone does. This is one of the reasons I have included Jean Delay's meticulous analysis of Gide's sexual nature, which might at first glance seem out of place in "a collection of critical essays." The remarkable way in which the essays of Knecht, Guerard, and Delay mutually reinforce one another is, I think, a strong demonstration of the validity of each. And all three bear out Maurice Blanchot's fundamental perception of the radical, the necessary role of the written work in Gide's great private gamble of a self-made and self-justifying life.

Everyone who writes of André Gide—even our Vatican critics— usually comes round sooner or later to talking of something called his "style"—most often last, as I am doing here. It is frequently added, in fact, as a kind of afterthought, an insincere gesture of homage to something ill-understood and not really admired, as if it were no more essential to him than the color of his eyes. The matter of Gide's style *is* essential, and insufficiently attended to in this collection—for the simple reason that this collection is intended primarily for readers of English, and whatever else style is, it is certainly untranslatable. But even the reader unable to savor the rigor, the nuance, the sensuousness, the occasional strangeness of Gide's French can appreciate, I think, Maurice Blanchot's demonstration of the crucial *moral* role that the right choice and placement of words plays in Gide's literary venture. He may even apprehend the justice and point of M. Blanchot's attempt to capture and to explain Gide's style, in a sentence that is itself no mean display of the resources of prose:

> For this slow and insinuating style he has chosen, with its apparently interior impulse, its progression at once indecisive and steadfast, reticent and enveloping, its ready yielding to the sensual qualities, the cadence of words (by which is counterbalanced the extremely studied and conscious elegance of his syntax), the mixture of effort and abandon, of precision and the appeal to uncertainty, of natural rigor and artificial hesitation, of warmth and ice, he knows perfectly how well it corresponds to the creature that he is, and that he has never really wanted to renounce.

IV

The question of Gide's continuing relevance or vitality was frequently raised in 1969, his centenary year. Gaëtan Picon, here, approaches it directly, Jean-Paul Sartre more obliquely. In one respect, every essay here, and the collection as a whole, may be regarded as addressing themselves to this question, insofar as they may challenge and help the reader to decide whether their subject still matters to him.

A decision for or against André Gide is, it seems to me, in the last analysis a very personal decision. All the issues raised by these critics converge to one signal fact: if Gide is to continue to matter at all in a serious way, it must be as a moral influence—as the sum of many moral influences—rather than as novelist, critic, stylist, or man of letters. And that is something that can only be decided by each reader for himself. He cared about the individual more than the community; many men, since Sartre, have regarded that as a criminal luxury. His humanism and optimism, as Picon points out, seem to many to be alien if attractive echoes from a past forever closed. "What moves us, what captivates us in Gide is, at least to some degree, the feeling that we are in the presence of a work the like of which we are not to see again—the belated and succulent fruit of a culture which is already beginning to take on the colors of a Golden Age. . . . Sometimes it looks to us like the last production of a freedom, a leisure, and a mental discipline that we cannot hope to recapture, so many and so fragile were the conditions that fostered them."

But the barriers suggested against Gide's durability—his individualism, his humanism, his optimism—are additional reminders of how private a matter one's basic response to Gide must be. One may still, potentially, be an individualist, a humanist, perhaps even an optimist, and thereby have something to learn from André Gide; or one may not. An "exemplary life" is really not something to be studied with impersonal detachment.

V

I am pleased to acknowledge here the gracious assistance of several Gide scholars, who kindly offered their suggestions for or comments on my table of contents: in particular Jean Hytier, Albert Guerard, Jacques Cotnam, Peter Hoy, G. W. Ireland, George Strauss, J. B. Barrère, Daniel Moutote, and Claude Martin. M. Germain Calmette, conservateur-en-chef of the Library of the Sorbonne, and M. Pierre Lafille generously made possible the extended loan of M. Lafille's unpublished *thèse supplémentaire* of 1953,

"André Gide et l'opinion en France de 1890 à 1950," which has been of considerable help. Had this book been twice as long, I should have included the essays of MM. Pruner, Stock, Vikner, Weinberg, Etiemble, McLaren, and Rivière noted in the bibliography, and I strongly urge the student of Gide to make use of them all—as well as the full-length works I have noted. This book depends, finally, on the resources of the University Library at Berkeley, California, and on the many hours spent there by Mr. Joel Kurtzman, my student and research assistant, finding and fetching works for me on André Gide.

The Living Gide

by Jean-Paul Sartre

They thought him sacred and embalmed. He dies, and they discover how much he remains alive. Embarrassment and resentment appear through the funeral wreaths which they grudgingly braid for him, to show that he displeases and will continue to displease for a long time to come.

He managed to array against him the union of reactionaries of the Left and the Right, and we can well imagine the joy of a few august mummies as they cried: "Thank you, Lord: Since I live on, it is thus he who was wrong." It suffices to read in *L'Humanité*— "A corpse has just died"—to realize how heavily this man of eighty-four, who scarcely wrote any more, weighed upon today's writing.

Thought has it own geography. Just as a Frenchman, wherever he goes, cannot take a step without *also* drawing nearer or farther from France, so also every movement of the mind either carries us nearer or farther from Gide. His clarity, his lucidity, his rationalism, his rejection of pathos, allowed others to hazard thinking in more obscure and uncertain areas. They knew, while on their voyage of discovery, that a luminous intelligence upheld the rights of analysis, of purity, of a certain tradition; should they be shipwrecked, the mind would not founder with them. All of French thought in these past thirty years, willing or not, whatever its coordinates may have been elsewhere—Marx, Hegel, Kierkegaard—must also be defined in relation to Gide.

For my part, I was too infuriated by the mental reservations, the hypocrisy, and not to mince words, the revolting stench of the obituaries devoted to him, for me to dream of emphasizing here the things which separated us from him. It is much better to recall the priceless gifts he bestowed upon us.

"The Living Gide." From Jean-Paul Sartre, *Situations,* trans. Benita Eisler, pp. 50–53. English translation copyright © 1965 by George Braziller, Inc. Reprinted by permission of George Braziller, Inc., and Hamish Hamilton, Ltd.

I have read from the pen of his contemporaries—whose gall has
never surprised me—that "he lived dangerously swathed in three
layers of flannel vests." What imbecilic scorn! These timorous creatures have invented a strange defense against the audacity of others.
They do not deign to acknowledge it unless manifested in every
domain. They would have forgiven Gide for having risked his ideas
and reputation if he had also risked his life, or to be specific, if
he had braved pneumonia. They affect not to know that there are
varieties of courage and that they differ according to people.

Well, yes, Gide was careful, he weighed his words, hesitated
before signing his name, and if he was interested in a movement
of ideas or opinions, he arranged it so that his adherence was only
conditional, so that he could remain on the margin, always prepared to retreat. But the same man dared to publish the profession
of faith of a *Corydon,* the indictment of the *Journey to the Congo.*
He had the courage to ally himself with the Soviet Union when it
was dangerous to do so, and greater still, he had the courage to
recant publically, when he felt, rightly or wrongly, that he had been
mistaken. Perhaps it is this mixture of prudence and daring which
makes him exemplary. Generosity is only estimable in those who
know the cost of things, and similarly, nothing is more prone to
move us than a deliberate temerity. Written by a heedless fool,
Corydon would have been reduced to a matter of morals. But when
its author is this sly Chinese who weighs everything, the book becomes a manifesto, a *testimony* whose import goes far beyond the
scandal which it provoked. This wary audacity should be a "Guide
rule for the mind": withhold judgment until the evidence is presented, and when conviction is acquired, consent to pay for it with
your last penny.

Courage and prudence. This well-measured mixture explains the
inner tension of his work. Gide's art aims to establish a compromise
between risk and rule, in him are balanced Protestant law and the
nonconformity of the homosexual, the arrogant individualism of
the rich bourgeois, and the puritan taste for social restraint, a certain dryness, a difficulty in communicating, and a humanism which
is Christian in origin, a strong sensuality which would like to be
innocent; observance of the rule is united in him with the quest for
spontaneity. This play of counterbalances is at the roots of the ines-
timable service which Gide has rendered contemporary literature. It
is he who raised it from the worn groove of symbolism. The second
generation of symbolists were convinced that the writer could only

treat, without loss of dignity, a very small number of subjects, all
very lofty, but that within these well-defined subjects, he could
express himself any way he liked. Gide liberated us from this naïve
chosisme:[1] he taught or retaught us that *everything* could be said—
this is his audacity—but that it must be said according to specific
rules of good expression—that is his prudence.

From this prudent audacity stem his perpetual turnings, his
vacillation from one extreme to the other, his passion for objectivity—one should even say his "objectivism," very bourgeois, I
admit—which made him even look for Right in the enemy's camp,
and caused his excessive fascination with the opinion of others.
I do not maintain that these characteristic attitudes can be profitable for us today, but they allowed him to make of his life a rigorously conducted experiment, and one which we can assimilate without any preparation. In a word, he *lived* his ideas, and one, above
all—the death of God. I can not believe that a single devout person
today was led to Christianity by the arguments of St. Bonaventura
or St. Anselm. But neither do I think that a single unbeliever was
turned away from faith by arguments to the contrary. The problem
of God is a human problem which concerns the rapport between
men. It is a total problem to which each man brings a solution by
his entire life, and the solution which one brings to it reflects the
attitude one has chosen towards other men and towards oneself.
What Gide gives us that is most precious is his decision to live to
the finish the agony and death of God. He could well have done
what others did and gamble on his concepts, decide for faith or
atheism at the age of twenty and hold to this for his entire life.
Instead, he wanted to put his relationship with religion to the test
and the living dialectic which led him to his final atheism is a journey which can be repeated after him, but not settled by concepts
and notions. His interminable discussions with Catholics, his religious effusions, his returns to irony, his flirtations, his sudden rap-
tures, his progress, his standstills, his backsliding, the ambiguity of
the word "God" in his works, his refusal to abandon Him even
when he believed only in man, all this rigorous experiment has
done more ultimately to enlighten us than could a hundred proofs.
He lived *for us* a life which we have only to relive by reading. He
allows us to avoid the traps into which he has fallen or to climb out

---

[1] *chosisme:* Sartre's own word, designating the rule of the thing (*chose*) or the
tyranny of subject-matter. (*Trans.*)

of them as he did. The adversaries whom he has discredited in our eyes, if only through publishing his correspondence with them, can no longer seduce us. Every truth, says Hegel, has become so. We forget this too often, we see the final destination, not the itinerary, we take the idea as a finished product, without realizing that it is only its slow maturation, a necessary sequence of errors correcting themselves, of partial views which are completed and enlarged. Gide is an irreplaceable example because he chose, on the contrary, *to become his truth*. Chosen in the abstract, at twenty, his atheism would have been false. Slowly earned, crowning the quest of half a century, this atheism becomes his concrete truth and our own. Starting from there, men of today are capable of becoming new truths.

The Death of André Gide

by François Mauriac

If, as M. Singlin said to Pascal, "the greatest charity we can show towards the dead is to do what they would have wished us to do while they were still alive"—then, we should spare a great writer who has just entered into eternal life the conventional flatteries of a funeral oration. One of his greatest claims to fame is that never, in the whole course of his career, did he once stop trying to be absolutely honest about himself. I shall not daub this dead man's face with paint. Imperfect Christian though I am, it is as a Christian—and it is what he would have wished of me, and expected from me, that I now meditate beside his grave. I do not pretend to have misunderstood the deadly lesson of *L'Immoraliste*— deadly for him, but also for us, in so far as we hearkened to it. If what Christians believe is true, then Gide knows now what all of us will know before long. What is it that he knows? What is it that he sees? When Lamennais lay dead, his brother wandered round La Chesnaie, sobbing out: "Féli, Féli where art thou?"

For Gide was very different from the picture most people had of him. He was the very reverse of an aesthete, and, as a writer, had nothing in common with the doctrine of art for art's sake. He was a man deeply involved in a specific struggle, a specific fight, who never wrote a line which he did not think was of service to the cause he had at heart.

What was that cause? It was firmly established on two levels. The most obvious, and in the eyes of the world, the most scandalous thing about it was that he had set himself not only to excuse, to legitimize, but even to recommend a certain way of love. But this was not the worst. Gide convinced only those who already shared his tendency. I do not believe that there was ever yet a hunchback who became one by persuasion. But this teaching of his was nothing but the application to his own particular case of a far graver determination, dating from his youth, which was to break with the moral law in its Christian form as taught by the churches.

The extremely important part played by Gide in my own life derived from this choice which he had made, without any attempt at concealment, at one definite moment, a choice no less spectacular, if I may say so, than Pascal's famous "wager." No one can ever have laid a bet against Christianity more calmly, more rationally, in spite of his moments of prudence, of his flashes of repentance, of his brief relapses. Such cases are far less frequent than one might think. Most men choose not to choose. Very few are prepared to take the hazard of deciding that evil is good, and good evil, to venture, as Bossuet says, "to overturn that tribunal of the conscience which has condemned all crimes." But that is precisely what Gide did, with a calmness, serenity and joy which makes the heart quail.

This was why his Catholic friends saw him as the apostle of Lucifer. Was it by mere chance that he lived at the centre of a furious spiritual battle? The conversion of Jammes and of Dupouey which led to Henri Ghéon's return to God, followed by that of Jean de Menasce, of Jacques Copeau, of Charles Du Bos, the exchange of letters with Claudel. . . . There can be no doubt about it, Gide lived in a whirlpool of Grace accepted, Grace repulsed. There were moments when even he seemed to yield, as when he wrote the ardent pages of *Numquid et tu.* But it was never long before he pulled himself together, and went off, striding down his own especial road, wrapped in his great cloak, with a terrible look of happiness on his face, valuing his joy above all else, that joy which he soon ceased to distinguish from pleasure.

A constant concern in matters of culture and of outward appearance, a perpetual effort, marvellously rewarded, to ennoble his particular type, his easy, distinguished, aristocratic carriage, preserved him from having to play the role of helot, which he left to other, lesser writers who came after him. We must have been living in a strangely unobservant age, ignorant of, or incurious about, contemporary trends, for the award to André Gide of the Nobel Prize not to have provoked a movement of amazement, even of terror throughout the world.

Gide's destiny has always seemed to me to have been shot through with the supernatural . . . like that of other men, you will say, but that I deny. For the most part, other men are just sinners, "poor sinners." Gide was not a poor sinner but a strange pilot, towering above a generation dedicated to "curious and gloomy errors," and holding the wheel in a powerful grasp.

What of his work? It is among the most significant of our time. This is not the place to study the influence of his critical thinking, which was embodied in *La Nouvelle Revue Française,* and the establishment of the true values which it set up. For me, *Les Nourritures terrestres, L'Immoraliste, Amyntas* can never wholly lose the charm with which the fervour of my twentieth year endowed them. But Gide, like Jean-Jacques and Chateaubriand, was one of those writers whose lives are a great deal more interesting than their works. They are at the very opposite pole from Shakespeare and Racine who vanish from sight in the radiance of their created characters. Like Rousseau's *Confessions* and Chateaubriand's *Mémoires d'outre-tombe,* and for the same reason, it seems to me that Gide's *Si le grain ne meurt* and his *Journal* will long keep active that ferment in the dough of humanity which it was their mission to provoke. . . . For evil or for good? On that point I will not commit myself: "All is Grace."

It is not for us to judge what God expects of a human being, of a human life. How is it possible to believe that a Nietzsche or a Gide were not intended to be what, in fact, they were? What happens in that moment of the gathering dusk, when the soul, on the very point of parting from the body, ceases to hear or see anything belonging to this world? During his last lucid moments, Gide may, perhaps, have remembered the words he wrote, not so long ago, in that short book which he dedicated to Charles Du Bos: *Numquid et tu.* "Oh Lord, as a child I come to you, as the child you willed that I should become, the child who gives himself into your hands. I resign all that was my pride, and, in your eyes, will be my shame. I listen, and to you I commend my heart." The man who was inspired to write that prayer, perhaps remembered it in the silence of his final hours.

"His most discriminating literary admirers like to forget that on five or six of the most important points in human thought, he was as positive and as clear-cut as any mind with a reputation for vigour and brutality." Those words were written by Barrès about Renan. What a revealing light they cast on André Gide!

That mind which wanted to be unbiased, did its best to be so, and believed that it was, about essentials, was nothing if not positive. It was this contrast which gave to it so great a charm. How readily did Gide bow to your arguments! With what feigned detachment did he leave you with the last word! But, left to himself, with his open note-book in front of him, he re-occupied in strength all the positions he seemed to have surrendered, passed over to the offensive, armed himself with all the concessions you had thought it good tactics to make, and turned them, with a sort of blunted fierceness against you, which did not matter, but above all against the truth you thought you had established. The *Journal* is filled with little else but those solitary and cruel reprisals at the expense of some interlocutor who had been so foolish as to think for a moment that he could get the better of an argument with André Gide.

He was charming, supple, sinuous, "kindly and gracious," ever ready to lapse into a softened mood, capable of being demonstrative, ready, on the slightest excuse, to be moved to tears, exquisite in conversation: these characteristics one cannot stress too often, because I can think of no other man with so keen an intelligence, who could combine it with what I can only call a quivering openness and sensitivity. But under all that grace and charm, there was a tautness of will, a clenched jaw, a state of constant alertness to detect and resist any external influence which might threaten his independence. A state of alertness? That is putting it mildly: beneath each word he wrote, he was carrying on sapping operations against the enemy city where a daily fight was going on against natural instincts, where the satisfaction of the passions was given the name of evil, where an especial curse was laid on pleasure, or what Gide regarded as pleasure.

Yet, this enemy city was still his city, the one where André Gide, the Calvinist, had been born into slavery, where, from youth up, he had suffered, and, with him, those many million human beings on whom the laws of the Christian City laid the same interdict.

There was a Spartacus in Gide. He was the leader of a slave revolt at the very centre of the Roman order. Spartacus was defeated after a short two years of rebellion, but André Gide, after half a century of constant victories, flung *Corydon* in the faces of bourgeois, priests and pastors, boasted in his *Journal* of a far greater number of exploits than Oscar Wilde had needed to make him acquainted with the dismal glory of hard labour, and, in return for all these provocative activities, got the Nobel Prize into the bargain!

It is by no means certain that, in his heart of hearts, André Gide did not look on all this success as in some sort a curse. He knew that the magnificence of Wilde and Verlaine had been paid for to the uttermost farthing. I have an idea that there were times when he wanted to be a martyr. I remember how, one evening, many years ago, he spoke to me with something like longing about the prison where Gustave Hervé had expiated his anti-militarist opinions. That, I think, showed Gide's greatness. It was no senile exhibitionism which led him to make the humiliating confessions which are to be found in his later *Journals,* but a desire to declare publicly that he had committed those same acts for which other men are still condemned and dishonoured. Never has the relativity of the moral code been so vividly displayed than in predicaments of this kind when the making public of a bad or even horrible act is occasioned by a demand for justice.

Beyond good and evil, this Spartacus led the way into the promised land of a new morality, at his heels those gangs of slaves who thought that they were breaking their chains, though, in fact, it was only Gide who achieved freedom. For him alone did this miraculous reversal operate. The ill-starred race to which he belonged got no benefit from it. To none of his disciples did he bequeath what he had enjoyed: all the gifts of the artist, a high degree of culture, maintained and enriched up to his dying day, an art of living deliciously at odds with a society on the demands and duties of which he had declared open war though without having to give up those comforts which it bestows on its more privileged members. To realize this, we have only to take a look at the younger, and far less distinguished representatives of this monstrous buffoonery of the western world, when they reveal in public the squalid secrets of the bedchamber, and perform indefinitely the hideous and joyless music-hall parody of the married state.

Inimitable Gide! With what feints and passes he always managed to ward off his heavily armed opponents! With what ease did he overthrow them one by one, and leave them sprawling in the clang and clatter of their Maurras breastplates, their Thomist panoply, while he, so nimble, in his Mephistophelian cloak and doublet (or was he not, rather, Faust, disguised in the devil's castoff clothing?)

stepped over their prostrate bodies, and hastened to his pleasures or his reading.

Virtuoso of the limited edition, of the book that is hard to come by, carefully cultivating his seeming unsuccess the better to ensure a more solid fame, it was, from the very first, on the fewness of his readers that he staked his money. In France, a land of peasant holdings and small shopkeepers, the gift of literary reputation is in the hands of three thousand discriminating persons. We no longer have a national literature. The *Nouvelle Revue Française*, Gide's own child, was the official organ of this coterie which could dispense rewards at will. Through it, he formed the opinions of us young men between 1910 and 1914. When I think back to those days, it seems to me incredible how many authors of all ages, from Théophile Gautier to Bourget and Henri de Régnier, he made us throw overboard. But how should we not have been fascinated and enthralled? It is a rare occurrence for culture and taste to reach so high a level in one man, who, moreover, was free of all ideological shackles. I have said that Gide, like Jean-Jacques and Chateaubriand, will live on only in those of his books which treat directly of himself: *Si le grain ne meurt* and the *Journal*, because it is he who interests us, and not the creatures of his invention. But I was forgetting that he remains the one and only subject of his imaginative books: *L'Immoraliste* is he: *La Porte étroite* describes the cerebral love on which he built the painful ambiguity of his life. All through *Les Faux-Monnayeurs* which, taken by and large, is a failure, runs the pulsating vein of Edouard's *Journal*. His presence in everything he wrote gives a lasting quality to his work.

Gide the virtuoso of dialogue: with his friends, with his adversaries, with himself, with Christ. He was the only one of our elders who had this remarkable gift. Barrès lived withdrawn behind his defences, a monster of indifference and inattention to everything that was not himself. Claudel; a Matterhorn at which one looked lovingly from one's window, but one cannot carry on a conversation with the Matterhorn. Jammes, sparkling with intelligence, a marvel of upward-leaping and spontaneous poetry . . . but having absolutely no understanding of others. With Gide, on the other hand, *how* one could talk, or, rather, how one could have talked if the first young man who came along hadn't always, unfortunately, distracted his attention. I never enjoyed anything approaching intimacy with him except during the few days when I had him, so to speak, under lock and key at Malagar, and twice in the course

of two ten-day periods at Pontigny.[1] When Gide formed an attachment he browsed on it at leisure, but it was the very devil to establish the attachment!

The old Ariel has now been dispersed to the elements, and his
going was his final gift to us. It administered a faint shock to the
small republic which drowsed away the time in the editorial offices
of the weekly press. "Ah! what a deal of interest will M. Renan's
death arouse!"—exclaimed the young Barrès—a piece of youthful
impertinence which conceals the greatest praise which an old writer
can be accorded by his juniors. Gide's death has not separated him
from us. Of him it cannot be said, as it was said of that same Barrès:
"Gide has wandered away. . . ."

It sometimes irritated Gide to feel all round him so many Christians on the prowl. At the same time, he enjoyed playing up to
them. But he attributed their relentless pursuit to what he held to
be a marked feature in their outlook, namely, a refusal to relax
their efforts until they had got the largest possible number of birds
into their net. Some of them did, in fact, give him good reason to
think that having the last word was all they cared about. I have
known several of these specialists in conversion who kept a "game-
book," and wore round their waists the scalps of the penitents who
had fallen to their gun.

But, if the Christians who were hot on Gide's heels had been
merely obeying the dictates of this infuriating mania, they should,
logically, have carried their activities into other fields as well. Yet,
I have never heard that Giraudoux, Jules Romains, or any other
libertine of letters was ever pestered by the convert-hunters.

There is no getting away from the fact that Gide's case was a
very special one. In the first place, it was he who had set the hunt
afoot, by which I mean that, having been born a Christian, and a
fervent one, at that, he had started an argument with what we
could not help feeling was a divided mind: had broken free from
all dogma, but not from the Scriptures: had become estranged from
his native Calvinism, but had fallen under the influence of the
Catholic affirmation, and was hesitating before taking the next step,

[1] Early in the twentieth century, Professor Paul Desjardins instituted, at his
home, the former Abbey of Pontigny, in Burgundy, a ten-day period every year
(the *"Decades de Pontigny"*) to which intellectuals from every country came to
discuss cultural, religious and other topics. These gatherings were a form of lay
retreat. (Translator.)

very much aware of those eddies of grace set moving all about him by the successive conversions of Claudel, Jammes, Dupouey, Ghéon, Copeau, Du Bos and many others.

The mystery of these several conversions, following hard on one another among men who were his familiars, was something, whether he liked it or not, which touched him nearly. This he did not deny, and *Numquid et tu* bears witness to the existence of a passing phase of fervour in this hero of our spiritual drama, from which he never completely withdrew till the day of his death.

Now yielding a point, now breaking off the action, he managed, almost to the end, by employing a high degree of subtlety, to maintain a firm stand against his Christian friends. He himself wrote in *Si le grain ne meurt,* speaking of the first time he took ship for Africa: "I made my farewell to Christ with so painful a sense of uprooting that I still doubt whether I have ever really left him at all."

This sense of uprooting was, from the Christian point of view, the basic cause of his essential error. Finding it as impossible to renounce Christ as to renounce himself, the only course left for him was to apply to his own case every word spoken by the Lord. It was a game at which he excelled. His *Retour de l'Enfant prodigue* is a masterpiece of evasion.

The first letter I received from him in April 1912 (dated from Florence) contained a violent protest against something I had written—I forget in what periodical—to the effect that *Le Retour de l'Enfant prodigue* had distorted the meaning of the Gospel parable. So obvious is it that this is so that I remember my astonishment when I realized that my words had deeply pained him. "I am writing," he said, "to protest with all the strength at my command against your use of the word *sacrilege* in relation to my *Enfant prodigue,* and against the charge you level at me of having stripped the Gospel parable of its divine meaning. I wrote those pages in a mood of piety and respect (is it possible that you have not *really* read them, or that having read them you have failed to grasp the emotional seriousness of which they are the expression?)."

The ambiguity here is obvious: as though the very seriousness of Gide's version of *The Prodigal Son* did not reinforce the distortion!

But the fact that he thought it necessary to protest was a sign that Gide the Christian recognized the gravity of the charge brought against his false parable. From the point of view of faith, nothing could more resemble what we mean when we talk of the "sin against the Holy Ghost." It is that which explains the violence shown by some of his friends, first and foremost by Claudel who had led the attack against him armed with the plumed helmet of hope, the tomahawk of faith, and the double-edged battle-axe of charity.

Gide's case was unique. The majority of Christians never get beyond the letter of the catechism. They have had no knowledge of God. It is a word which, for them, has never had any real content. They deny, yet do not deny. Christ has never been in their lives, as he was in that of André Gide, the friend of whom Lacordaire speaks, whom once we met on our road when we were young, who has loved us and been by us beloved. They have not taken the trouble to make him say what he did not say, before turning their backs on him. If we are agreed that only those will be forever lost who have deliberately renounced God, in full knowledge of what they were doing, and as the result of a choice long weighed and considered, then I do not remember ever having come across a more glaring instance than that of Gide.

It goes without saying that in the Christian view only God can judge the reasons which determined Gide's attitude, some of which were, beyond all doubt, deserving of respect.

True enough, but this is no place to mince words. The fact of the matter is that Gide's particular form of erotic satisfaction lay at the very centre of his drama. The struggle he waged was about that and about nothing else. For him the point at issue was the legitimization of a special type of desire. This, in itself, is not the attitude of a base or vicious mind. Gide's standard was a high one, in that it implied the need to be in a state of complete and perfect balance, which meant that he was to refuse nothing, to deny nothing of the contradictory aspirations of his nature as its deepest level. But nothing can alter the fact that this demand, made by himself to himself, was bound to result in that reversal of standards for which there is no forgiveness: "evil be thou my good." That was precisely the situation which Gide was busy formulating when he wrote *Le Retour de l'Enfant prodigue.* The adulteration of the Parable led him to undertake a basic subversion.

Here it is necessary to dwell upon the special nature of Gide's character. Christ in his teaching seems to take no account of personal tastes. It is not his concern to know the bizarre inclinations of this or that individual. His commandment—and this is true for all of us—is—that we be pure, that we renounce our lusts, *no matter what their object may be.* The world's condemnation of homosexu-

ality operates on the social level and has nothing in common with
Christ's condemnation of *all* defilements, nor with the blessing he
has accorded to those who have kept themselves pure: *Beati mundo
cordi quonian ipsi Deum videbunt*. Many pure hearts have strangled
in themslves a tendency which Gide not only excused, but approved
and glorified. What it comes to is that he was demanding special
treatment for one especial vice. Remembering the words put by
Pascal in the mouth of Christ: "I love thee more fervently than thou
hast loved thy filth," [2] my conclusion is that Gide loved his filth above
all else, but first of all denied that it was filth. And here, for the
believer, there intervenes another aspect of Gide's life—the angelic.

To make it possible for agnostics to understand the interest shot
through with pain which Gide's case aroused in his Christian friends,
I will quote, without comment, three passages (though I could find
many more of the same kind). The first two are from Gide's own
writings. One occurs at the beginning of the second part of *Si le
grain ne meurt,* where he says: "Though I have recently come to
think that an important actor, the Devil, played a part in the drama,
yet I shall relate that drama without, in its early stages, referring
to the intervention of one whom I identified only much later." The
other is an extract from the *Journal des Faux-Monnayeurs*: "There
are days when I feel in myself so massive an invasion of evil, that
it seems as though the Prince of Darkness were already establishing
hell within me."

The last I take from Julien Green. Describing, in a quite recent
publication, Gide's behaviour to him, he says: "After my return to
France in 1945, I never met Gide without his trying, in one way or
another, to attack my faith."

Don't misunderstand me: from the Catholic point of view there
is nothing in those passages which should make us despair of the
salvation of a friend whose reasons were never base and often dictated by concern about the less obvious points of moral teaching,
and when one would least have expected it of him. Thus, for instance, certain admissions in the last volume of his *Journal* are
introduced for the sole purpose of showing that the very same acts
committed by him, dishonour other men, and that he had been
privileged not to share their fate: he demands his share of disgrace.
Never was there a case which called upon us, with such good reason,
to remember the precept: "Judge not!" and Saint John's words,

---

[2] H. F. Stewart's translation.

when he says that the Lord came among men not to judge but to save.

I have tried, here, to do no more than try to cast some light on the reasons for that sort of blundering busy-bodying of which André Gide's Catholic friends were guilty during his life. Not that I regard myself as being less of a sinner than he was. Far from it! Gide was never a "poor sinner": he stood erect and triumphant, the very image of defiance.

Condemnation of the Works of André Gide

Supreme Sacred Congregation
of the Holy Office

Decree: Proscription of Books

Wednesday, April 2 [1952]

In the course of the general assembly of the Supreme Sacred Congregation of the Holy Office, the Most Eminent and Most Reverend Lord Cardinals charged with the safeguarding of the faith and morals, after the vote of their reverend lordships the consultors, have condemned and ordered to be entered in the Index of Forbidden Books *the entire works* of ANDRÉ GIDE.

And the following Thursday, April 3, 1952, His Holiness Pius XII, by divine Providence Pope, in the regular audience granted to the Most Reverend Monsignor the Assessor of the Holy Office, approved, confirmed, and ordered to be published the resolution of the Most Eminent Fathers which had been handed over to him.

Given at Rome, at the Palace of the Holy Office, this 24th day of May 1952.

MARINUS MARINI, notary for the
Sacred Congregation of the Holy
Office

Remarks of L'Osservatore Romano:

The severity of this *post mortem* condemnation may seem, today, unexpected and terrible, but this is due to its irreparable character.

"Condemnation of the Works of André Gide," from *L'Osservatore Romano*, June 1, 1952. Copyright 1952 by *L'Osservatore Romano*. Reprinted by permission of the publisher. Translation by David Littlejohn.

The author dead, his work now rests immutable, fixed in its final aspect; in a certain manner, it is fixed forever, as the features of the author grew rigid in death.

By his Protestant origin and character, no less than by the warm and constant friendship of Catholics, among whom his wife was the first,[1] André Gide lived in the bosom of Christianity almost uninterruptedly, from his birth to his death; but it was always as a non-Christian, nay more, as a committed anti-Christian that he dwelt there. A tendency towards profanation, sometimes in a tone of childish titanism, sometimes in a tone of perverted pietism, was pushed by him to the point of blasphemy. The last pages written by him before his death not only breathe the air of vice and abound in horrifying remarks aimed at Catholics; they are also filled with sarcastic denials concerning Christ. He would have done better to have kept silent—no more to have chosen vice for his subject than to have chosen Christ Himself; but *always* to be wallowing in the mud, constantly to soil the purest thing in human history, which is the figure of Christ and the love men have for Him, *this* he calls sincerity. And it is clear that he suffers from a kind of furious and glorious compulsion to be "sincere" in this peculiar way. No one has ever spoken so frequently of "responsibility," nor with an irresponsibility so pronounced that it seems diseased and irreducible. It is with stupefaction that one sees how, in his last pages, even to his very last page, he persists in his customary obscenity, which leads him to write such incredible things: "I have never said so much on this subject; but it seems that the more is said on this matter, the more there is to say." It was literally "hard for him to stop." Death arrived unexpectedly, finding him where his friends always used to find him, at the same point, saying the same words over and over, like a broken record, like a man demented, like a man obsessed, like a man unpunished and incorrigible. "On our arrival in Algiers," he himself relates confidentially in certain horrible posthumous pages, "the two of us alone in the omnibus that was taking us to the hotel, she [his wife] finally said to me in a tone in which I felt even more sorrow than censure: 'You looked like either a criminal or a madman.'" Exactly: and this is precisely the judgement the Church declares on him today. It is true that the wife of Gide, as early as 1926, had become so much a Christian that her husband dared to write these very words in his

---

[1] [Mme Gide was never a Catholic.]

journal, amidst pages of the most pathetic disgust: "The slow progress of Catholicism on her soul: it seems to me that I was watching the spreading of a gangrene." He watched the growth of Christianity in his wife, and compared it to that of a gangrene.

This, then, is André Gide. We must, finally, characterize and denounce his particular poison: the pleasure he took in feeling himself reproved (see his constant reflections on it); in corrupting, soiling, affirming what decent men deny, and denying what decent men —even at the cost of their lives—affirm. To walk with a limp, and insist that that is the best way to go: to know oneself to be hunchbacked and to boast of it, and to laugh at those who are straight. All this without the least energy or courage, other than the energy it takes, if one may speak so, to be weak at all costs, other than the courage to proclaim one's fear in the face of all the world. He *made* of his sin a coefficient (and not the least) part of his fame. Above all else he delighted to find himself at the center of his dear friends' entreaties, just so that he could scorn their prayers and cause them pain. He placed himself and kept himself in a scandalous situation, one that could assure him the only gladiatorial role a man like him could permit himself: that of a hero of depravity.

A gifted writer, of fine expressive skills, one of the most renowned, his very art reeks of his lasciviousness, impressed as it was into the service of the latter vice, like a chambermaid who dresses and adorns her mistress. Gide's work is marked by the imprudence that became his special trait (and that of his imitators), an imprudence which spreads itself immodestly over every page; it is, moreover, from beginning to end, orchestrated in a tone of equivocal seduction, a tone so obsessed that one ends up disgusted and nauseated. He appears like a kind of impotent Racine, cold, sometimes bored. His music seems, on first appearance, to be something superior; but it is bent and adapted, most often, to such a degraded inspiration, to his ever-renewed perfidy, to his impure sterility.

When we consider what the Christian literature of France has been, and precisely during Gide's own lifetime; when we think how many great writers France has given us, animated both by a Christian faith and by high poetic feeling, we cannot but lament the destiny of a man like André Gide, who was no less gifted than they, nor less renowned. He liked to play the Prodigal Son. He delighted in hearing himself called, just so that he could refuse to answer the call. All this he thought quite charming of him, and never once realized that there is no joking with God. He even took every precaution to make his death itself into a demonstration against God ("to do without God . . . those who wish to never succeed"); a fresh insult against Christ ("Christ, in believing, and in making us believe that he was co-responsible in all things with God, was deceiving himself and us"); a new negation of the faith that moves mountains—"Yes," said he, "mountains of absurdities"; a new sneer at his Catholic friends, affectionate, broken-hearted friends, friends like Jammes, Claudel, Ghéon, DuBos, Mauriac, to name but a few. He succeeded; and he died as he lived, in a spirit of negation.

He could not succeed, however, in getting away from the foot of the cross. He may not be standing with the two Marys, but one could always find him there—even if it be with the executioners. The Lord may well have granted the prayers of so many of his loving friends, and forgiven him; but the Church can do nothing else but place him among those who have themselves elected as their only companions the executioners of Christ—no longer now on Calvary, but in the hearts of men.

To crucify Christ and to persecute the Church: and to do this in these years when it has been so necessary to unite men rather than to divide them, to gather them together and not to disperse them. The celebrity of Gide, so slow in growing, ended by filling the whole of the last forty years, and not only in France. Generations of young people have submitted to his impure seduction. Thanks to Gide, things which until now would have been whispered in the ear among adults have become something to boast of—to boast of indecently—among adolescents. He himself invented a way of refuting Christ by borrowing choice phrases from the Gospels, even quoting them in Latin in the manner of musical motifs, of attacking the Church from within the sacristy or presbytery itself. It was with pleasure that he found himself outdoing the profane in his profanity, that he played the gnawing worm—one that gnawed on the Cross, on the Crucified Christ. Thus it was that he was responsible, precisely by means of a *reaction* against such disgust, by means of an irresistible and imperious nausea, for provoking and accelerating the conversions of a great number who had never been Christians, and for stirring up new flames of faith in those born in the fold. But the higher the flames of faith burned around him, the more he froze. The last image of Gide, a pale old man without a fire to warm himself by, is enough to chill one to the bone: he looks like one of the lost.

Poet of the most suspect joys, of the vainest of glories, he never quite managed to extinguish totally in his heart the Christian vocation; to it he returned over and over, to wound or mutilate or mislead it. In spite of the foul odor that arises from his elegant and diseased pages, he was not entirely corrupted, for he was still able to write, in memory of his wife, the two passages that follow:

> What is our love made of, then, I used to wonder, if it persists in spite of the crumbling of all the elements that compose it? What is hidden behind the deceptive exterior that I recapture and recognize as the same through the dilapidations? Something immaterial, harmonious, radiant, which must be called soul, but what does the word matter? She believed in immortality; and I am the one who ought to believe in it, for it is she who left me. . . .

> Yet however different from me she may have been, it was having known her that made me so often feel like a stranger on this earth, playing the game of life without too much believing in it, for having known through her a less tangible but more genuine reality. My intelligence might well negate that secret reality; with her, I felt it. And in the absence of the pure sound that soul gave forth, it seemed to me thenceforth that I had ceased to hear any but profane sounds, opaque, faint, and desperate.

From that moment on, in fact, Gide became more and more violent. He did not simply move towards death, he hurled himself toward it. And despite the pious ceremonies today, disgusting revelations, accusations of deceitfulness and worse pile one after the other atop his recently-dug grave. The Church cannot keep silent long; the work of this writer deserves to be condemned both for what it affirms and for what it denies. Let it, therefore, *be* condemned, in no uncertain terms. The gift he had received, a gift of profound intelligence as well as poetic riches, renders this condemnation all the more pitiable, but also all the more necessary. In the manner of his own dearest friends, the Church waited till the last minute for the return of the Prodigal Son. He never came back. Let his place be marked, at least, in the Christian militia, as among the enemies and corrupters; let his place be fixed among the partisans of the Adversary. At a time when the easy and shifting spirit of doubt, in the press, in the schools, even in politics, is dissolving, destroying faith in men's hearts, and under the pretext of laying everything open to vigorous argument is only undermining and devastating all; André Gide, with a power and a sweetness of voice that at moments recalls the loftiest voice of France, *dared* to reduce to a state of open question the one thing we have that is most certain, most secure, most worthy of respect—and *not*, be assured, to return and reaffirm it with greater force and originality, but in order to deny it, shamelessly, and to doom himself shamelessly in so doing: worse, to make of this act his fame, his profit, and his reward.

The Presence of André Gide

by Gaëtan Picon

Thesée has just come to remind us that André Gide remains in our midst as something more than a distinguished survivor. It was perhaps to be expected that this little book would provide us with an example of perfection, of the art of composing and writing not soon to be equalled; but what is more surprising is that the presence from which it radiates has lost nothing of its former power. Not for a moment do we dream of greeting it with that chill veneration one reserves for classical monuments, as one more volume to add to the Collected Works, which we may now feel free to have bound and to put to sleep on our bookshelves. *Thesée* speaks to our present lives, our uncertainties, no less than to our formal sensibility (which disdains to give any special privilege to contemporary values). *Thesée* brings to us the latest creative act of a magnificent life's work, the late and perfect fruit which has been ripening patiently for twenty years; and, at the same time, a priceless, vigilant voice which has its place in the present dialogue.

It is the special quality of great and powerful works that, in concerning themselves with nothing *except* themselves, they provide answers to the very questions we want to ask. This is their inimitable secret: attentive only to themselves, they remain works one never interrogates in vain. From *Le Voyage d'Urien* to *Thesée,* Gide's work has developed as if according to a plan of timeless logic, untouched by external events. Never has it deviated or bent under pressure from outside. Gide has submitted to influences, there is no doubt, and, as he justly says in the latest notebooks of his *Journal,* one of the deficiencies of *Si le grain ne meurt* was his not having

"The Presence of André Gide" (original title "Actualité d'André Gide"). From *L'Usage de la lecture,* by Gaëtan Picon (Paris: Mercure de France, 1960). Copyright © 1960 by Mercure de France. Reprinted by permission of the author and the publisher. Originally published in 1946 as a review-essay on *Thesée* and the 1939-42 volume of the *Journal.* Translation by David Littlejohn.

acknowledged them. And there has been, certainly, an evolution in his work. But he seems to have drawn these influences out of his own private depths. Never have they acted upon him as external pressures, shaping his features from without. We ought to see them as nothing more than certain fixed points that he not only chose himself, but even shaped to his own order and size. Gide is the sole director of his own evolution. Of the only truly external shock to which his work has ever submitted (the discovery of the social question[1]), it is now clear how little his writing was really changed by it in the long run. One might know nothing of what had taken place, in literature or in history, between 1890 and 1940; all he need do is review Gide's very first works in order to understand *Thesée* completely. Had it all taken place differently, the adventures of our mind, the avatars of our existence, Gide would still, setting out from the same premises, have arrived at the same conclusions. All things considered, the work of no author is more inflexible and less dictated than Gide's, so uncertain, so hesitant, so apparently susceptible to each wind that blows. But the hesitations come only from within, he himself secretes whatever it is that troubles and divides him. There is no work less circumstantial, less "committed" to anything external. At a time when the writer, if he is not asked to "serve," is at least expected to attend to present circumstances and to reply to the questions of the moment, there is no one who upholds more firmly than Gide the classical identification between what is valuable and what endures.

The miracle is that these qualities of endurance are no hindrance to present relevance. No doubt any position sufficiently profound contains within its own limits all that can be found *outside* of it—and that universality of significance is part of the very nature of a masterpiece: that inexhaustible ambiguity which allows us to read it according to the demands and direction of our own disquiet, as (depending on the particular bias that inspires them) people see the most diverse shapes in certain patterns arranged in order to achieve that effect.

So this work that once seemed dated remains astonishingly near to us still. But is not its "untimeliness" still quite intact, for all that? André Gide has not ceased to assert the supreme value of form, at a time when the best of our literature is tempted to see

[1] "If I had encountered that great trap at the beginning of my career," Gide avows, "I should never have written anything worth while" *Journal*, May 30, 1940.

in it no more than a simple means of expression, of which one may
insist that it be wholly transposable and translatable. To a generation that sees the work of art as an adventure or a revelation, much
more than a patiently-constructed edifice, Gide recalls the willful
composition of the classical work. It is not unintentionally that he
crowns his work with this *Thesée*—he who, with *Les Caves du
Vatican* and *Les Faux-Monnayeurs,* has given us the example of
several modern myths; it is as if he wanted to prove that the great
traditional myths still retain an incomparable power of suggestion.
What could be more unlikely in our day than this recourse to
classical mythology? For to some, nothing matters but sheer invention; to others, nothing but what has been snatched and stripped
bare from everyday reality.

But a myth, for Gide, is not just one of the games of imagination.
It comes to us charged with a deep human meaning; but one that
has need, precisely, of the *indirection* of myth if it is to shine forth.
It is this usage of myth, its very superiority in the realm of human
knowledge that Gide displays in setting his *Thesée* (where he reveals nothing of himself except by hiding) against his *Journal*—in
which we may well believe that he has endeavored to eschew all
fiction. But what is it, then, that the myth has to tell us?

No more, it would seem, than the man—no more than an individual. By the indirection of myth, in *Thesée,* or without it, in
the *Journal,* what is made clear is that the sole ambition of André
Gide is the perfect possession of all that is human, through the
agency of himself: that eminently classical proposition, the knowledge of Man, as reseen through the perspectives of a modern
individualism—Rousseau added to Pascal. The concern for the
enquiry, for the documentation itself becomes exclusive of all other
concerns. "For it is first a question of understanding properly what
one is," as Theseus says to Hippolytus.

But this is no longer our concern. The preference accorded the
non-fictional enquiry over the novel strikes us as quite natural, but
Man is no longer the same thing for us that he is for Gide: the
interior, individual creature. Having abandoned the shores of difference, we have taken up residence in the *common*: it is there,
according to our faith, that the true Man is to be found. No longer
do we think that Man can define himself by means of his interior
life; he is to be captured, we rather believe, in his formal and exterior existence, in his social situation, in his metaphysical role.
Man, in many recent works, could be any man—the most replace-

able of all beings.[2] We are concerned less with what Man knows, feels, believes, than with what he is—a Man implacably shaped by his place in time, his relation to the universe, his actions and decisions, his reflection in the eyes of other people. Abandoning the classical algebra of emotions, our literature no longer wants to be a literature of introspection, of psychological analysis; the individual himself has been effaced from the sky of contemporary literature (psychological individualism survives only in extreme, almost monstrous works, falling back into the fringes of the human landscape after having reigned so long over the center), along with the old description of him. In place of the old inventory of a conscience, we are now offered the description of a situation. Man is still and always our problem; but his self-knowledge seems to us rather to dissolve his image than to shape it. It is from *outside* that he must be apprehended: in his actions, in his choices. Here we have Malraux saying that man is what he does, not what he hides; there, Sartre affirming that nothing else is possible except what exists, and that an action is not the manifestation of an emotion, but the emotion itself—both of them orchestrating the same decisive transformation of the human spirit. Human reality has gone far beyond those vague ripples that Narcissus spied when he leaned over his own reflection.

On the other hand, *Thesée* serves up to us once again all the "Gidean" problems—and it is fair to regard this book as, if not the masterpiece, at least perhaps the most complete expression of its author. When Theseus, impatient to assume the throne, forgets to put out the white sails on his ship, we hear again the old "Families, I hate you . . ." *Passer outre;* to go beyond—this is the imperative that governs the hero in all his adventures, his labors, his perils and amours; it is also the law of *L'Immoraliste,* and that of *La Porte étroite.* One can recognize here all of Gide's temptations. Theseus saved by Ariadne, then betraying Ariadne—what is this but the old confrontation between freedom and fidelity, adventure and order? Icarus defeated and Theseus triumphant—the struggle between prudence and excess. The seductions of the Labyrinth— constructed, Daedalus informs us, "in such a way not that one cannot . . . but that one does not want to escape"—are those of the passing moment; and the death of the Minotaur is the victory

---

[2] [An allusion to Gide's *Les Nourritures terrestres,* in which he exhorts the reader to make of himself "the most irreplaceable of beings."]

over those seductions. And finally, Theseus against Pirithoüs,
Theseus against Oedipus—this is the affirmation, against pessimism
and uncertainty, of a humanism that believes in man's perfectibility
—and that terrestrial existence offers us all the meaning we need.

I wonder, though, whether it would not make more sense to
speak of Gide's *position,* rather than of his debates and uncertainties.
Gidean "indecision" is a commonplace, but perhaps one less well-
founded than is generally believed. For are there not, in the last
analysis, other constant qualities in Gide's makeup than discontent
and agitation—as well as a good number of positive assertions that
he has never really seriously questioned, and which are more than
enough to regulate the whole of one's life and work? It has always
seemed to me that Gide's work was an instance of a *centered* work,
a life's work built entirely around a perfectly firm and constant
attitude; and *Thésée* only serves to confirm this impression. That
Gide's thought is not something simple and unsubtle does not
imply that it is necessarily indecisive. That he is able to entertain
a contrary opinion, understand it, respect it, perhaps even envy
it does not mean that he identifies it with his own. No doubt he
does proceed by a form of dialogue, refusing to stifle brutally the
voice of his adversary; but it is no less true that his own voice
is always to be found on the same side of the dialogue. What we
take for indecision, is it not rather a simple respect and consideration
for the ideas of the opposition (so easy is it to confuse assurance with
ignorance and incomprehension)? What seems a contradiction, is
it not rather a tendency to reunite under a single attitude personal
qualities more commonly dispersed? I think it inexact to present a
Gide torn between the hedonism of *L'Immoraliste* and the first
Nourritures, and the austerity of *La Porte étroite,* between the
seductions of the Labyrinth and the determination to conquer the
Minotaur. Did not he himself describe *Nourritures terrestres* as a
"Guide to Self-Deprivation"? Did he not tell his reader to throw the
book away? The idea of momentary pleasure has never been for
Gide an absolute, an acceptable resting-place. "Go beyond" is still
the highest law; if it crosses the pleasure principle, it is the former
that takes precedence. "Do not think of finding rest except in death,
your destiny achieved," is Daedalus' advice to Theseus. Sensation
is nothing but a moment in the limitless development of oneself,
and to stop at that point would be to betray the greater exigence that
aroused it. By conceiving of them as parallel paths, Individualism
becomes for Gide a way to Humanism, far more than an absolute

in opposition to it. It will be answered that Gide has no sense of incompatibles, that it is useless to try to reconcile the irreconcilable. But that is not the question. What is true is that Gide does not think from the point of view of the irreconcilable, and that this tendency of his mind allows him to choose one thing without brutally rejecting another.

I do not want to imply that Gide identifies himself consciously and fully with Theseus. But neither do I believe that Theseus corresponds to nothing more than one of his thousand contradictory possibilities, as people are wont casually to suggest, and that it would have been just as easy for him to depict himself as Oedipus.[3] Because in the last analysis, if Gide seems to hesitate, it is more between a choice of means than between a choice of ends. Torn between order and adventure, between tradition and progress, between man and mankind, between fidelity and freedom, between prudence and daring, between self-indulgence and self-denial, Gide cherishes, in all cases, one single wish: that of presenting (as he says of Goethe) an exemplary image "of what Man can attain on his own, without any recourse to Grace." "I have fulfilled my destiny," says Theseus; "behind me, I leave the city of Athens." I leave my writings, Gide is thinking. There is one certitude free from all shadow of doubt: on the condition that we do not let the opportunities it offers us escape, on the condition that we act according to our own highest law (the one most difficult to follow), human life, life confined to a this-worldly horizon, possesses all the meaning we require. Gide's sensibility to Christianity is a moral one, in no wise religious. There is doubtless no unbeliever closer than Gide to Christian values; but very few of those who reject these values, with however great a passion, are quite so totally closed to the Christian metaphysic as he is. He puts this very clearly himself in a page of his most recent *Journal*.[4] When Oedipus appears before Theseus, I cannot believe that Gide feels himself for one moment on the side of Oedipus. No doubt he understands Oedipus better than Theseus does, but to know another person in this way does not imply the least complicity. "I remain a child of this earth," says Theseus; as does Gide. He has never for a moment stopped believing that the only life we have is the one we lead on this earth—and that it is quite sufficient; that the true light

[3] As, for example, Armand Hoog asserts in a recent review in *La Nef*.
[4] Page 21.

is the one that shines in the day, not that which emerges from darkness, that which can be seen only with the hollowed blind eyes of old Oedipus; that human will, demanding of man the fullest self-realization, has no need of waiting for "heavenly aid" to give meaning to this life below; that our destiny is not to be enlightened, pardoned, and saved from without; that each man carries his own redemption in himself. Gide has nothing of the Christian sense of guilt, of all life stained by Original Sin. With regard to what lies beyond the earthly horizon—the eternal, the invisible—he feels neither longing nor anxiety. There is no one more firmly planted in time and in visible reality than Gide, the very image of restlessness. How many pages of his *Journal* could one not quote as commentaries on the dialogue of Oedipus and Theseus! When Gide writes, "that would be gay, wouldn't it, always to be faced with the immutable?" [5] I frankly cannot detect the accent of deaf agitation one traditionally expects to find in such declarations. Gide's "acquiescence" is as serene, as complete as it could possibly be: much closer to Goethe's than to Nietzsche's. And his great sadness in these latest notebooks from the *Journal* is due not at all to the fear of death, but to the regrets of old age—the remorse of a magnificent life that he still feels to be insufficiently full.

It would seem that Gide conceives of no other conflict but that between religious discontent—which refuses to concede that our life has any sufficient meaning of its own, and sets against it a deep dissatisfaction, a constant appeal towards things beyond—and humanist acquiescence, which accepts man's earthly state without the least shadow of regret, without any vain longing after the impossible. It is to religious transcendence that Gidean humanism is opposed—and this humanism seems to be an attitude simply taken for granted. But such assurance, such humanistic serenity is more classical than modern. The image of man that Gide offers us is more reassuring than exalting, more wise than it is splendid: an image, fundamentally, quite near to the optimism of the eighteenth century. Theseus believes in progress; he has no fear of using against Pirithoüs that somewhat dented weapon. I do not know whether Gide believes in social progress, after his brief communist experience; but he certainly believes in the indefinite perfectibility of the individual. His underlying idea is that man's natural condition is an acceptable one, and that it is up to us to make the most of it. For Gide,

human misery is unnecessary and avoidable—man's unhappiness
depends less on the fatality of his nature than on the poor use he
has made of it. Here we are not far from Rousseau: Society and
History come along and disturb a State of Nature created for
happiness. "That man was born for happiness—surely this is what
all nature tells us," said the first *Nourritures*—and despite the griefs
of our particular time, the author of these latest *Journals* has not
forgotten that truth. "Radiant midsummer days," notes Gide on
July 19, 1940,[6] "on which I constantly repeat to myself that it is
entirely up to man to make it beautiful, this miserable earth on
which we are all devouring one another."

All this rings very little of today. For it seems quite true that one
of the great discoveries of modern thought is that of the profound
and ineluctable character of human tragedy. In the world of action,
tragedy does not spring from chance, from social artifice, from
human folly: it is the necessary result of the existing conditions of
our present society—or more inexorably still, of the very nature of
society itself. In the domain of human existence, tragedy is implicit in our situation in the world. In the very place where we
have seen the face of God, the image of Reason effaced, there
emerges now the vision of an absurd world, opening onto Nothingness, where abandoned man wears himself out in useless gestures.
Today it is this tragic image of man that sets itself against the
religious view, so much so that religion, which strikes Gide as
something shot through with uncertainty, seems to us security itself.
Gide does not share the modern sense of the Absurd, and it could
be said that our problem is the reverse of his, since for us the
issue is one of getting beyond the natural agony of our human state
and finding again if not satisfaction, at least a justification for life,
however tenuous and fragile it may be. What is for Gide a natural
point of departure, the regular dwelling-place of his thought, is
for us a distant and improbable horizon towards which we are
mournfully making our way.

In great part, the value of Gide's work is coexistent with its
lack of contemporary relevance. There is in this nothing surprising:
it would be absurd to believe that we can admire only the things
that move in our own direction. We are never so wholly satisfied
with ourselves that we are not quickly tired of our own concerns.

[6] Page 67.

What we are is as much the result of pressures as of choice. The "non-contemporary" will benefit from that seductive attraction we feel towards things we have left behind: the potent nostalgia of time past. What moves us, what captivates us in Gide is, at least to some degree, the feeling that we are in the presence of a work the like of which we are not to see again—the belated and succulent fruit of a culture which is already beginning to take on the colors of a Golden Age. We love to puzzle out forgotten secrets in it, the traces of a lost happiness. Sometimes it looks to us like the last production of a freedom, a leisure, and a mental discipline that we cannot hope to recapture, so many and so fragile were the conditions that fostered them. It looks to us, too, like the final example of a truly classical work—I mean a work that is before all else *crafted,* constructed at the same time that it is written, the issue of a writer patiently working in his own unique style, and thereby identifying a particular moment in the history of the language. The work of Gide is the expression of neither a system of thought nor a fixed personality: it is first and foremost the search for, and the elaboration of, a style. Neither Proust nor Valéry produces such an impression. Their work does not allow us to observe this gradual birth of a form; it does not allow one to penetrate inside the artist's workshop. Their style is the expression of a nature already fully-formed. It is, in itself, an absolute. The relationship between sensibility, biography, and finished work in Proust, between the thought and the written work in Valéry, is that between the thing to be expressed and the expression of it. In Gide, what we have is a more intimate, reciprocal, shifting relationship between two realities, each of which is transformed in acting upon the other. His work is at least as much the creation of a style as the expression of an established ego—and the style is the history of a personality that is in a parallel process of transformation. There is a young, a mature, and an old style in Gide, because his own youth, maturity, and old age are present in his work. The greater part of his contemporaries' works have an odd sense of fixity, resolution, definiteness. His own is perhaps the last instance we have of a collected work that can profitably be studied in chronological order, with distinctions drawn between successive stylistic and philosophical phases. And one may well wonder whether this is not one of the signs that a cultural revolution has definitely taken place. Because what this intimate relation between life and work in effect implies, if one studies it closely, is the attribution of a kind of incommensurable value to the work of art—since every stammering, every slightest variation in the life is willingly confided to the work, since the transposition into art suffices to validate all things. One may well believe that there will in future be few examples of a life that puts so high a value on the work of art that it is perfectly willing to be itself indistinguishable from it.

But the absence of contemporary reference does more than merely seduce us into turning nostalgically towards the past. It has also the value of representing an always-possible future. If we live to outreach our present state, the moment always comes when this outreaching begins to look like a return to the past. Each new way soon reaches either its saturation point or its end, and we must therefore be willing to regard each metamorphosis as a possible restoration. Not only does each new adventure tend to arouse the need for order, but even more: each adventure—that of the Pléiade, that of the Romantics, that of the Surrealists—was in part a return to the past. It is quite possible that the work of Gide will very soon acquire (has perhaps already acquired?) a kind of posthumous relevance, which will allow us to make use of it against ourselves, as its *living* relevance once allowed us to make use of it as a weapon against Symbolism, Naturalism, or traditional moralities.

When we grow tired of probing our metaphysical condition and examining ourselves from the outside as some kind of mundane object, the work of Gide will be able to recall for us the still-unblemished richness of the moralist tradition. Against the external and unitary image of man towards which we are tending it will set the value of the internal and the distinctive. Not that Gide's writings (however much they may be nourished with the subtle lyricism of a private interior life) are representative of the literature of introspection—not at all. Sartre's strictures against Proust, for example, could never be applied to Gide. A classical writer, devoted to the study of man, he never made use of psychoanalysis. For aesthetic reasons, first of all: believing as he did in an art of suggestion and secrecy, Gide has always been shocked by the excessive clarity of analysis, by its exhibitionism, by the fact that it reduces to nothing the contribution of the reader. It says everything; it says too much. Secondly, it always seemed to him more easy to describe sensations and ideas, to note them in passing, than to gather them up and categorize them; art begins on the other side of analysis. But there are deeper reasons too. Gide is perfectly aware of the illusory character of introspection; in fact he was probably the first man to understand it. The ambiguous, vague, at bottom inconsistent, ultimately non-existent nature of the interior self— when considered as a substantial reality one is trying to describe, independent of the mind that is observing it, as a chemical reaction is independent of the chemist—this was hardly to be lost on the man who said that he could see no difference between what we feel and what we imagine we feel, the man who wrote, even more explicitly, "I am never anything more than what I think I am." Which can only mean one thing: that there is no such thing as a true interior being, already formed, waiting for us to come and uncover it; that we are *not* something made, but something-in-making—the image that we believe in and want to be. One should speak not of self-consciousness, but of a consciousness of one's self-image, of a dream, a desire, a will, an interpretation of oneself. This is why Gide does not write *Maximes* and why he is unwilling to stake his all on the *Journal* by itself. Knowledge of man, for him, is inseparable from his moral formation, which is why he makes use of the fictions of *Les Faux-Monnayeurs,* the *Caves,* the myth of *Thesée,* instead of naked and direct observation. It may well be Gide's mission to remind us at one and the same time of the value of moral understanding and the significance of indirection and hypothesis—both of which today's literature, awakened from its fictional past, has dangerously cast aside.

In these terms it would no doubt be useful to specify the exact place of the *Journal* in the Gidean *oeuvre.* He is not to be judged on the basis of the *Journal,* any more than one judges a text by its commentary. But the *Journal* of Gide is far less an exercise in understanding than an exercise in self-development. Its subject is not the description of a personality in itself, as if it existed prior to this sounding he is making of it (which, as we have seen, is pure nothingness, or at best a summation of insignificances)—but precisely this sounding, this appeal itself. We see André Gide as someone ever working towards the development of himself. This the the rich and fruitful image he offers us; not that of some pure and absolute being. Gide reproached Chateaubriand for having, in his *Memoires d'outre-tombe,* assumed an attitude; but taking the word in its deepest sense, what else is he himself doing in his *Journal*?

We have said that his life's work is before all else the elaboration of a style; Gide himself insists that it be judged solely from the aesthetic point of view. But it *is* also an attitude, proposed for our observation: an example of a way of life. It remains to be seen what likelihood there is that André Gide will become again, in the future, one of the "directors of our conscience."

I shall limit myself to saying that present circumstances are such that what yesterday seemed to be illusory or inadequate may tomorrow appear to be a salutary truth. Gidean individualism may have stood in the way of a concept of man more general and more useful; his taste for nuance, his perpetual state of dialogue may have threatened the need for order to which we aspired. But is the scene never going to change? The order, the simplification, the unanimity we longed for are so nearly achieved that we can now see that none of them is exactly what we had in mind. In fact it is in opposition to this simplification, this abolition of all dialogue and all nuance, that we are tempted today to reassert the values that seemed archaic such a short while ago. And I do not mean that it is sufficient to fight Order with individualism, anarchic liberty, the suffocating plurality of previous years; I mean that this Order will prove fruitless and inviable if we are not allowed to find in it the better part of the endangered wealth of diversity—which is precisely what Gide can help us to do.

I should make the same remark concerning another characteristic of the Gidean mind, that anti-historicity that the writer himself has confessed to in his *Journal* [7]—thereby excusing himself for the uncertainty (and often the naïveté) of his judgments, for which he has been so vigorously and so vainly attacked. Lately we took this as proof of his limitations, his increasing age; but may not this tendency soon appear to be the sign of a renewed youthfulness in his work? Not long ago history seemed to us an inspiring myth; now it has taken on the colors of the Apocalypse. Not long ago history offered us a notion of man from which it seemed useless to try to escape, outside of which, we thought, there was nothing but illusion and inconsistency; now it has become a bondage and a threat. From now on, is not our problem precisely one of establishing a sufficient *distance* between history and ourselves? It is worthy of note that a thinker like Malraux, more sensible to history than any other, more ready to identify man and his epoch, has come, in his "Colloque de l'Altenburg," to affirm a human permanence that defines the limits of history and provides man with an efficacious means of

[7] To which, he says, he owes his disposition to happiness, but which can "lead to serious inconvenience" (page 93).

protection. It is this same concern for the preservation of man in history that has united minds as different as Albert Camus and Roger Caillois. Sartre himself has only abandoned the concept of human nature to rediscover a sufficient stability in that of the "human condition"; he has accepted the notions of engagement and revolution after having reserved, on the side of subjectivity, the claims and the place of a *philosophia perennis.* It is natural that the generations who have discovered history are now obliged to measure themselves against it in the name of mankind. We are forced to consider man in his immutable nature, subtracted from the determinism of coincidence, if we are ever to attribute a value and a meaning to his existence. If this is our problem, we should not hesitate to return to André Gide, both because he has always proposed to us the example of the essential and the permanent, and because he has affirmed more highly than anyone else the virtues of freedom.

Gide and the Concept of
Literature as Adventure

by Maurice Blanchot

Anyone who has tried to observe in a spirit of fairness the work and person of André Gide must have been struck by this primary characteristic: it is almost impossible to speak of this body of work *except* unfairly. If one looks intently at an isolated aspect of it, he is neglecting the very thing that is important about that aspect—the fact that it is *not* isolated, and that it admits the truth of the opposing aspect as well. If one underlines in his work this affirmation of contraries, he is forgetting the tendency to equilibrium, to harmony and order which has ever been its animating force. It is a work of excess, and a work of perfect proportion; completely devoted to art, and yet shaped by the quest of a moral influence, an influence not in the least aesthetic; a work more important than the man, and at the same time a work that was only one of the means of development for the creature who made it, made it by living, and in order to live, and without sacrificing anything of himself; a work immense, in the long run, and of extraordinary variety, but also thin and narrow and monotonous; open to the richest culture and confined to the most un-bookish spontaneity; naive, by reason of its love of effort; free, thanks to its concern for constraint; discreet in its frankness; sincere to the point of affectation; and driven, so it would seem, by restlessness toward repose, towards a kind of serenity in which nothing would ever change.

It is generally admitted that the *Journal* is the work that represents him best. But why? For it is also agreed that his most finished works, those in which he has most assuredly approached perfection, are *L'Immoraliste, La Porte étroite, La Symphonie pastorale,* short, perfectly composed *récits,* utterly foreign to the limitless movement that is driving the *Journal* towards its happily unforeseeable conclusion. These *récits* are flawless things. *Les Caves* and *Les Faux-Monnayeurs* are regarded as "failed" works, but the influence of these imperfect works has been considerable—*too* powerful, even, when one considers that their affective power is temporarily exhausted, and the very novelties they authorized and made possible make them appear old-fashioned today. On the other hand, the "treatises," which have never been wholly successful—with the exception of *Les Nourritures terrestres*—and for which this demiobscurity is perhaps appropriate, continue to exercise a profound influence; in any case, they are responsible, every bit as much as the far stronger works of Lautréamont and the surrealists, for the obligation felt by contemporary literature to be *more* than literature —to be a vital experience, an instrument of discovery, a way for man to test himself and, by means of this test, to strive (in vain) to outreach his grasp.

Gide, through his work and through the very way in which he joined it to his life, gave a new signification to the word *essay.* We can, of course, find his predecessors throughout our literature. But this hardly matters, since it is precisely *he* who illuminates the relationship, in giving to the writers to whom he is related the new meaning that justifies such an affiliation. One could say that he has created those from whom he is descended, and that they owe to him all that he owes to them, which is precisely the value of what we call culture. As early as 1893, speaking of *La Tentative amoureuse,* he wrote in his *Journal,* "I wanted to suggest, in the *Tentative amoureuse,* the influence of the book upon the one who is writing it, and in the very course of that writing. For in emerging from us, it changes us, modifying the course of our life. . . . This is consequently a means of acting on oneself *indirectly* that I am suggesting here; it is also, more directly, a story." A preoccupation of his early youth? But thirty years later, going back over the whole of his work, Gide was to write again:

> It seems to me that each of my books was not so much the product of a new state of mind as its cause, on the contrary, and the original provocation of that mental and spiritual disposition in which I had to keep myself in order properly to elaborate the book. I should like to express this more simply: that the book, as soon as it is conceived,

disposes of me wholly, and that, for its sake, everything in me to my very depths tunes up. I no longer have any other personality than the one that is suitable to that work—objective; subjective? These words lose all meaning here; for if it happens that I use myself as a model (and sometimes it seems to me that there can be no other exact way of painting), this is because I first began by becoming the very one I wanted to portray (*Journal,* 1922).

The last remark in this quotation has to do with the art of fiction, which, dominated (no doubt incorrectly) by the idea of the character, has given rise to so many conventional critical reflections. One of these conventions is that the novelist is a writer capable of bringing to life separate beings, free and distinct from himself. This is not the place to investigate all the problems this assertion gives rise to, nor how very difficult it is, to tell the truth, even to understand what it means—if one is interested in taking it to a more than superficial level. But let us note that when one attributes to literature the power to create a life different from that of the creator, it is most often done simply as a means of expressing one's admiration for the freedom of the work of fiction; rarely does one recognize *in* this freedom the means the author has discovered to involve (and to risk) the sense of his own freedom. We are shown the spectacle of an author locked in battle with his own heroes, yielding to them, overcome by them: Jarry *becoming* Ubu. But this hypothetical "drama" is of little real interest because of its oversimplified notion of a character—a character here understood as a personality, a fixed temperament assimilated to a particular object. Art, though, from the point of view of the artist, a novel from the point of view of the novelist, and, in a more general manner, the very fact of writing from the point of view of the one who writes—these are a quite different thing: a vital and dangerous experiment in which one is risking his very self, putting himself to the test.

> For a long time, for too long a time (yes, up until the last few years), I tricked myself into believing that I was mistaken, that I was wrong; to accuse and contradict myself; to shape my way of seeing, of feeling, and of thinking to that of others, etc. I seemed to be afraid of my own ideas, and for this reason I felt obliged to assign them to the heroes of my books, in order to put them as far away from me as possible. Certain people refuse to acknowledge that I am a novelist, and per- haps they are right, because it is this that leads me to the novel, rather than the telling of stories.

When Gide notes this in his *Journal,* we can see in his remarks a concern for making literature serve as a veritable experiment: an

experiment on oneself, an experiment on one's ideas: not in order
to preserve and confirm them, still less in order to win others to
them; but to detach oneself from them, to set them at a distance,
to "try" them by confiding them to another existence—that is to
say, to misrepresent and decide against them. Of course, André
Gide's "experiment" was too often a test of his ideas alone, and
not of his existence; which is why he is able to be unfaithful to his
own inspiring impulses. For there is no real experiment except when
(as he himself very nearly says) everything—and all of one's self—
is set at hazard. But insofar as he *has* followed this impulse (and
in spite of the very scruples which led him to accept the objections
of critics, for whom the only true novelist is the teller of tales and
the creator of characters), he has been not only a great writer of
novels, but also one of those who has contributed in giving to contemporary literature its essential character—that character which
allows us to call *Maldoror* a novel, *Nadja* an admirable novel, in
the same terms as the works of, say, Malraux—who is also a great
creator of "experimental" novels.

It is a simple thing to assert that literature is an activity through
which its adepts tend not only to produce beautiful, interesting,
and instructive works, but also to test themselves absolutely; not
to tell their own stories, to express themselves, not even to discover
themselves, but to follow through an experiment in which the thing
sought for is the whole sense of the human condition, as it can
be known through oneself and the world one has. It is easy to repeat
that writing has, for the writer, the value of a fundamental experiment; we go on saying it, repeating it, but in the end all we are
repeating is a formula, void and illusory; prodded by examination,
it simply eludes the effort of criticism—on the integral value of
which it nevertheless insists. One of the qualities of Gide's work is
that of helping us understand these difficulties, in that it is itself
made *out* of them, out of the internal debate they have provoked
in Gide. Nor have his works triumphed over these difficulties, but
rather accepted them, tested them with a willingness at once dis-
contented and jealous, in the very real pain of being unable to
surmount them, and the satisfaction, having found them insurmountable, of having drawn from them the occasion to fascinate
his infinite curiosity and spirit of inquiry.

From the moment the writer writes with the secret awareness that
by what he is writing he is "disposing" of himself "completely,"
the terrible question of the demands that may reasonably be made

of "art" is posed with dramatic seriousness. The case of André Gide is particularly illuminating in this respect. A product of the Symbolist school, he never renounced his faith in the idea of perfection, in the virtues of a finished form and a fine style. The major part of his existence as a writer is dominated by a desire to live in accordance with the ideal of a true and harmonious art. For Gide, to be faithful to the act of writing well does not imply that one must be unfaithful to or betray anything else; it means to follow the road that leads the farthest, that makes possible the most important, the boldest adventures. Why? An act of faith, based on a centuries-old cult and the example of the masters. In his mature years, instructed by experience, Gide could still write: "It is very difficult for me to believe that the wisest, sanest, most sensible idea is not also the one that, projected into prose, yields the most harmonious and beautiful lines" (*Journal,* 1928). The elegance and harmony of a felicitous structure are not then mere aesthetic satisfactions that the author allows himself, as a kind of reward for yielding to his own talents. What is hoped for goes far beyond that: it is the assurance that, when all has been put in question, the shape and structure of his sentence will remain as the measure and safeguard of its value. "I wanted to make of my prose an instrument so sensitive that the mere displacement of a comma would be enough to destroy its harmony" (*Journal,* 1931). "The demands of my ear, up till these last years, were so great that I would have bent the meaning of a sentence in the interests of its rhythm" (*Journal,* 1923). Eager to be sincere, the young Gide questioned himself on the meaning of artistic sincerity, and defined it in these terms: "I hit upon this: the word must never precede the idea. Or else: the word must always be necessitated by the idea. It must be irresistible and inevitable; and the same is true of the sentence, of the whole work of art." Between these two assertions, that of sincerity in his youth, that of "good writing" from his later years, there is no contradiction, but rather a profound accord. *Be perfectly sincere,* demands the Gide of 1892, and the other Gides reply in full faith: All right, then; write in conformity to the innate harmonies of the language, and in such a way that once the phrase is traced, once the work is finished, all the resources of the language will not permit the least word to be changed.

Always more audacious, but less skeptical in all matters than Valéry, Gide is *infinitely* less so on the question of the truth of art and of rhetoric. Valéry sees the means and effects of art as nothing but arbitrary and conventional, and it is because he denies any substantial value to form that he accepts and insists on its strict limitations: the only "perfect" writer is the one for whom perfection, of itself, has no meaning. But Gide is never so impious. Art, in his eyes, does signify something; writing a work is not a simple exercise: to write well is to give truth the greatest possible chance to be told, to give oneself the greatest possible chance of telling the truth, without yielding an ounce of one's boldness. If one begins to question the power of language, the value of rules and form— whether traditional or not does not matter; if one writes "I believe that everything must be questioned" (*Journal,* 1931); and if one does not retain an intimate confidence in the very words that introduce this grand questioning: then one is left with only two choices— either to become the author of masterpieces in which he does not even pretend to believe, or to lose oneself in the dismal repetitions of noiseless chatter. Valéry decided in favor of masterpieces, and in the end the masterpieces got the better of his skepticism, reducing it to the state of something relatively inconsequential, something brilliant but rather ineffectual.

The possibility of negation in Gide, less radical than Valéry's and, for that reason, more profound, less easy to quell, led him to an extraordinary confidence in the resources of culture and of literary art—no doubt too great a one. For it does not appear that his desire to write in order to leap into the unknown, or in order to do battle against himself—a desire he once wrote of in a letter to Francis Jammes[1]—ever led him to give up the ideal of writing *well,* nor even to any internal conflict between the former desire and the exigencies of the finished, crafted work, able to stand the test of time. Still, it is entirely possible that to write well may be, for the one who is writing, the best way to risk and to test himself; but the reverse is possible too. In reproaching Pascal for his overly-refined phrases on the misery of man, Valéry means to imply that Pascal's own misery, if it had been more honest, could never have expressed itself in language so fine. But why not? This is what is not clear. For in the very line in which Valéry detects a "fine style," a style too sure of its effects, too anxious about achieving them,

---

[1] "Can you not understand that I despise my own ideas? I am in the habit of fighting against them, but I cannot deny my ideas but by means of . . . my ideas, as one casts out devils by Beelzebub, prince of devils (which I tried to demonstrate, moreover, in *Paludes*); and this only strengthens them." Cited by J. Hytier, *André Gide,* Editions Charlot.

Pascal would perhaps have seen no more than the expression of a falling-off, a lapse, which he felt compelled in all anxiety to discover in himself. Nonetheless the question remains open. Indeed, we have seen great writers who gave off writing altogether; we have seen others who discovered their own barrenness by means of the richest language, or who tormented themselves with the consolations of superb imagery; but we have never seen one who, continuing to write, forced himself to write badly, who ruined his own talents by means of his talents, under the impulse of a genuine experiment. After *Phèdre,* Racine kept silent; he never contemplated writing another, a second-rate *Phèdre* like Pradon's. And had he become another François Coppée instead of the merchant of Harrar, who can say whether Rimbaud would ever have become a seer, a *voyant* —or have spent his true "season in hell"? And if "it is with fine sentiments that bad literature is made," as Gide says, then by coming down to bad literature, he who is capable of better may well be lifting himself, surpassing his own limitations more genuinely than by following his natural inclination—which is to produce great works that posterity will preserve.

Gide was often troubled by "fine writing," by great literature, and we should never forget it. It seemed suspicious to him; at one and the same time he served it with great faith and observed it with defiant suspicion. The sincerity on which he interrogates himself— from his early youth on—often comes in conflict with the demands of good prose.

> The desire to compose the pages of this journal deprives them of all worth, even that of sincerity. They do not really mean anything, never being well enough written to have a literary value. In short, all of them take for granted a future fame or celebrity that will confer an interest upon them. And that is utterly base (*Journal,* 1893).

And, twenty years later, "Perhaps, after all, my belief in the work of art and the cult that I make of it prevent that perfect sincerity which I henceforth demand of myself. What interest have I in any limpidity that is nothing more than a quality of style?" Sincerity is an excellent weapon to use against the rights of literature—even of language itself. Sometimes it attacks it for saying too much, for saying more than is true ["that amplification of the emotion, of the thought, of which *good writing* so often consists in French literature" (Journal, 1931)]. Sometimes it dismisses it for its simplicity: to say anything at all is always to say too little ["If I stopped writing in it (the *Journal*) for a long time it was because my emotions were becoming too complicated; it would have taken me too long to write them down. The necessary simplification made them less sincere; it was already a literary restatement . . ." (*Journal,* 1893)]. Or, as we have just seen, it may even hold against it its *limpidity,* that is to say, its tendency in some respects to be too *pure,* of too perfect a transparency—a very serious objection, and, for classical art, quite fatal, since it presumes that confused emotions can be justly expressed only by phrases that betray them, that convey them *without* clarity, without decorum, without that minimum of order that exists in anything true. Whence arises the temptation not only to write without style, but to write *against* all style or against oneself, to expect from something written spontaneously, for example, the expression of a greater sincerity, as if speed, the absence of reflection, and "naturalness" could offer greater guarantees in this regard than patience, study, and that second naïveté which is achieved only by taking pains.

Sincerity is an admirable principle from which to argue. Nothing contents it: neither naturalness, which is simply the lie of the first impulse; nor artifice, which is a satisfied acquiescence in deception; nor banality, which is a yielding to the bad faith of the majority; nor the cult of "differences," which would save the impostor by regarding him (deceitfully) as unique. Silence itself is false, because it is nothing more than language ignorant of itself—a language which, moreover, by that very renunciation of language, expresses itself all too clearly. "I am torn by a conflict," writes the young Gide, "between the rules of morality and the rules of sincerity. Morality consists in substituting for the natural creature (the old Adam) a fiction that you prefer. But then you are no longer sincere. The old Adam is the sincere man. This occurs to me: the old Adam is the poet. The new man, whom you prefer, is the artist. The artist must take the place of the poet. From the struggle between the two is born the work of art" (*Journal,* 1892). But why should the new *preference* be any less sincere than the former state? On its side there is the truth of desire, the richness of what is yet to come; in it there is promise, there is life; facticious it may be, since it has to do with a creature not yet made—but, by that very token, less falsified by usage. Moreover Gide himself, later on, will take back these affirmations, and find the true *naïf* beyond the merely "natural," the reward of effort; find sincerity something to be obtained, to be conquered and not just inherited.

Art is a delusion, as Mallarmé says; and this is why sincerity is so valuable an adversary to it—an adversary which would possess all the attributes of a supreme and universal rule, were it not in itself an imposture. Whence derives the discomfort that accompanies all its judgments, whence the fact that it falls victim, of necessity, to its own condemnations. "The word *sincerity* is one of those that are becoming harder and harder for me to understand. . . . In general, every young man thinks he is sincere when he has convictions and is incapable of criticism" (*Journal*, 1909). Gide, before Freud, gave careful thought to the deficiencies and excesses of sincerity, and even before he came to Marx, he was to judge insufficient that twisted authority, distorted by the blindness of the inward-looking eye which proclaims itself as pure and knows nothing of either history or the world. But it was, in fact, at the moment when he first took serious account of social problems that he most categorically took his leave of art and seemed willing to see it disappear.

> That art and literature have nothing to do with social questions and can only, if they venture into them, go astray, I remain almost convinced. And this is partly why I have been silent since such questions have become uppermost in my mind. . . . I prefer not to write anything rather than to bend my art to utilitarian ends. To convince myself that they must be uppermost today is tantamount to condemning myself to silence (*Journal*, 1932).

And this in July 1934: "For a long time it can no longer be a question of works of art."

It seems to us that this challenging of art in the name of a hoped-for objective liberation, and in conformity with the necessities of this struggle for liberation (which renders *all* other activity negligible, at the same time that it denounces the insurmountably mystifying character of art)—that it is one of the most serious burdens that can be imposed on an artist. The debate between André Gide and communism was the most pathetic moment of his existence, his supreme moment, the moment that demands our most serious attention. And even if we put aside here the question of which are of greater value, his "retouches" or his early enlistments, we ought still to recognize that this encounter was for Gide like an encounter with a wall—a wall he could neither pass over, nor accept as final, nor ignore, before which he had to content himself with a backing off, all the while feeling that retreat was not the answer. A political man, let it be said, may "turn Communist" and then turn away; for him, this phase may or may not be of great importance. But the writer's

case is different. He may withdraw from such a confrontation, even
for the strongest of reasons; but he does not withdraw intact; something in his vocation has suffered a mortal wound. He allowed his
vocation to be questioned and attacked—once—and thereby granted
it to be questionable. And the arguments that he used against it
then continue to render it suspect to him now—as an activity whose
cost he now sees in the very satisfactions it affords.

But in the case of Gide, one cannot but see with what precautions,
with what *reticence* rather, he accompanies the words "there can no
longer be a question of works of art," from the very moment he first
utters them. Why is art abandoned? Because it does not want to
"bend [itself] to utilitarian ends"; it is sacrificed *in order that* it may
be kept pure. There may well be in this world a task more important
for a writer than writing; Gide recognizes this in all seriousness, and
is quite willing to accept the consequences; his ears are assailed by
lamentations altogether too pressing, and he has no inclination to
make others listen to him. So he will condemn himself to silence. An
extreme sacrifice, yes; but all the same, it is not only the sacrifice of
literature to the world's distresses, but just as much the sacrifice of
art to itself, of an art that cannot acknowledge ends higher than
itself in the existing order of values, cannot acknowledge alien laws
that would only serve to corrupt it. So the defeat of art is at the
same time a victory for art, which shuts itself in silence and retires
until a later date.

But there is more to the artist's obligation than this. To write no
more, if the interest of mankind wills it—so be it; but insofar as one
does write, to write well, to write in accordance with the principles
of good writing, considered apart and in themselves, as one can per-
ceive them in the enclosed sphere of literature, because they of all
rules are the least deceptive, the most likely to help the man who
writes to express more than himself, more than he knows—in a
word, to create. The *Journal* is, from one end to another, shot
through with stylistic torments. "I no longer like things written
slowly. This notebook, like all the other 'journals' I have kept, is
designed to teach me to write rapidly." "These pages seemed to me
much too 'written,' too lacking in spontaneity." "I have just reread
the last chapter of my Memoirs, which I promised myself to write
straight off, and over which I have already taken such pains. I find
nothing of what I wanted to put there; everything strikes me as
studied, subtle, dry, elegant, faded." Just as "vice" became virtue for
Gide, insofar as virtue was natural to him and the abandoning of it

an arduous conquest of effort, so also, too naturally tempted by elegance and the precautions of language, yielding with excessive facility to the exigences of rhythm (to the point where he looked to the *measure* of a line for its truth and its meaning), he sought to forbid himself this indulgence, and force improprieties into his diction, errors into his syntax (*Journal*, 1914); and above all to write quickly, write in advance of, one step ahead of himself, through a veritable act of anticipation and discovery. In this regard, his scruples are not only those of a writer whose tastes were to become more and more classical, who was to learn to prefer the sharpness, the precision, the dryness of a line to its music. This discontent, this uncertainty regarding form is equivalent to an uncertainty also with regard to the very value of the experiment one is making by writing. Why does Gide repeat so often the line from Stendhal's *Armance*: "I spoke much better once I started beginning my sentences without knowing how I was going to end them"? Because it represents for him that mysterious and dangerous gesture that the act of writing is for the one who writes, who begins a sentence without knowing where it will lead him, who undertakes a work in total ignorance of its conclusion, who feels bound to the unknown, engaged in the mystery of a process greater than he is, and through which *he* becomes greater than he is, a process in which he risks losing himself, losing everything, but also finding more than he was looking for.

But at the same time, such a preoccupation does not invalidate the rights of style—far from it. It reinforces them; its concern is with the very essence of proper language. "I spoke much better. . . ." What is at stake here is always the same thing—the matter of proper speaking, proper writing considered as a law; what it is, at last, that Gide admires in Stendhal is "that element of alertness and spontaneity, of incongruity, of suddenness and nakedness, that always delights us anew in his style." He admires this style and regards it as a good model to follow. But insofar as it is a question only of a style, and not of a way of seeking, a means of discovery, it is inevitable that however excellent he may hold Stendhal's to be, he is not likely to stop preferring his own. For this slow and insinuating style he has chosen, with its apparently interior impulse, its progression at once indecisive and steadfast, reticent and enveloping, its ready yielding to the sensual qualities, the cadence of words (by which is counterbalanced the extremely studied and conscious elegance of his syntax), this mixture of effort and abandon, of precision and the appeal to uncertainty, of natural rigor and artificial hesitation, of warmth and ice, he knows perfectly how well it corresponds to the creature that he is, and that he has never really wanted to renounce. He knows how much this kind of good writing, so common and so rare, resembles himself—insofar as a tendency to escape from himself (but only up to a certain point), to assume other roles, is part of his character, and the very act by which he affirms his own character and assures himself of its existence. "It will not be a simple matter to trace the trajectory of my mind; its curve will be revealed only in my style, and many people will not see it."

The "only up to a certain point" is Gide's secret. Whether one is considering him as an artist, as a creator of forms, or as the witness and creator of his own life, as the man who, while he lives, lives charged with desire, at once wholly immersed in the life he is leading now and already beyond it, wholly at the disposition of whatever adventure he is giving himself to, but never driving it so far as to bar him from any other, he always ends up by discovering, at the very brink of self-forgetfulness, the moment that brings him back to himself; at the extremest point of innovation, the guarantee of some traditional rule; in his moment of greatest risk, a longing for, a sudden taste for propriety and balance. The century has been such that, for one whole part of his life Gide saw himself rejected because of his audacity; for another, because of his *lack* of audacity. But what has happened is that the century has learned from Gide his own intrepid curiosity for extremes—but not his patience, nor his honesty, nor his faith in the work of art, nor his spirit of prudence and, as he calls it, of parsimony. And this is why his example remains ambiguous and mysterious. Some will see him as (and reproach him for being) an author too sure of himself, an author who, even though he writes to "set all things in question," writes also in order to "put something out of reach of death" (*Journal,* 1922); who would very much like to be an unbeliever, but without going so far as impiety; and who, as soon as he touches the extreme limit of an experience, is afraid of losing hold of himself completely and hastens to pull himself together, to regain his self-control ["Need to tie the circumference to the center. It is time to go back" (*Journal,* 1912)]. To these critics, one may justly reply that Gide's boldness is a function of his prudence, that his *inquiétude* is all the more meaningful because of his longing for rest, that his earnest desire for emancipation is all the more valuable, coming from a mind incapable of disrespect or disdain for religion. But at the same time we should remind ourselves that if the essential qualities of Gide are patience within impatience, reserve within excess, propriety within abandon (the impulse to break the rules), then true discretion for him would have been to give in completely; absolute propriety to break all the rules, hopelessly; the most fruitful kind of patience to live with no thought for the morrow, far from all notions of fame, all subtle schemes of "influence," which Gide has enjoyed so and served so disinterestedly, and which are repaying him today by the most extensive and most honorable renown.

When we see Theseus come out of the Labyrinth, the glorious victor in his single-hand combat, we are right to suspect a certain trickery or illusion. For there is no labyrinth except for the man who subjects himself to it; and the trial is not real except for the man who does in fact get lost; and the man who gets lost cannot come out to tell us about it—to tell us, "It is easy to go into the labyrinth. The difficult thing—there is nothing more difficult—is to get out. Nobody finds his way in there unless he loses it first." [2] Because Gide's Theseus knows how to retrace his steps, because he is marvelously prompt at transforming the fiery passion of Ariadne into an enchantment he can control, he will always be open to these suspicions: the suspicion that he never really entered the labyrinth—because he managed to get out of it; the suspicion that he never really encountered the Minotaur—because he was not devoured by it. There is no way out of the dilemma. Theseus finds his way out because he kept himself tied to something sure, but since he never broke the thread, he can never be said to have *known* the labyrinth. To which he can reply that the man who does not come back has ventured less far than he did, and that no one can truly be said to have "lost his way" *except* the man who has never relinquished his sense, his understanding, his love of the straight and narrow.

Literature is a dishonest and devious adventure in which one never succeeds unless he fails, in which "failure" means nothing, where the greatest scruples are suspect, where sincerity becomes a farce; it is an essentially deceptive adventure, and it is this that gives it whatever value it has, because he who writes enters into the realm of illusion. But this illusion, in deceiving him, leads him forward, and in leading him forward by means of the most ambiguous impulse, gives him, according to his taste, the chance either to lose what he had believed himself already to have found, or to find what he will never again lose. Gide stands as a meeting-place of two conceptions of lit-

---

[2] *Thesée,* Editions Gallimard.

erature: that of traditional art, which sets over everything else the pleasure of producing masterpieces; and that of "literature as adventure," which laughs at masterpieces, and is prepared to destroy itself in order to attain the inaccessible. From this position comes Gide's double destiny. As a model of literary honesty, he is regarded for years as the prince of equivocation, as the devil himself. Then the immortality of the classics discovers him. He becomes the greatest living French writer. And fame reduces his image to that of a mere sage.

Le Voyage d'Urien

by Albert J. Guerard

Le Voyage d'Urien (1893) has had few readers and almost no commentators; it demands a much fuller analysis than Gide's other early works. For this earnest prose-poem is one of the most tantalizing of Gide's works, psychologically, and its literary and historical interest is much greater than that of *André Walter*. One notable advance is that Gide can now look at his aspirations to purity with an occasional ironic smile. The twelve pilgrims who resist the seductions of Queen Haiatalnefus are a little ridiculous, their chastity somewhat pompous: "Slowly then the twelve of us, in state and symmetry, hieratic in our sumptuous apparel, descended toward the sun, even unto the last step where the broken waves drenched our robes with foam. . . . Nobility of spirit constrained us to make no gesture, to keep silent. . . ." [1] And the change from the diary of an adolescent in a solitary room to a symbolist journey to the North Pole and its divine city already shows some progress toward objectivity. The voyage is a "voyage du rien" (Mallarmé had feared it would be the account of a real trip), yet contains everything. It is a Homeric *Pilgrim's Progress*, replete with sirens and other perils of the sea: a dream of life as a series of embroidered and sensuous dreams, and as the puritan rejection of those dreams. A verse palinode admits that the author might have resisted all Urien's temptations, but had been subjected to none of them. His book nevertheless comes as close to being a novel as anything French symbolism would produce. It represents the extreme limit to which Gide would go to

[1] All quotations are from the admirable translation of Martha Winburn England, written for my Harvard seminar on the modern novel. . . . Mrs. England was helped by Mr. George Steiner on the first draft of the translation.

satisfy the symbolists who had adopted him, and writing it perhaps
hastened his sharp reaction—to the irony of *Paludes,* to the earthy
hedonism of *Les Nourritures terrestres.* Yet even the student of
Gide's later style must take *Le Voyage d'Urien* into account: its lux-
uriant rhythms and exotic descriptive riches, its nebulous appeal to
the fringes of the reader's consciousness. These vague harmonies and
uninhibited translations of soul into landscape had to be exploited,
before the progressive chastening of style could begin.

As a Symbolist novel, *Le Voyage d'Urien* stands somewhere between the occult reality of *Arthur Gordon Pym* and the cloudy
philosophizing of Novalis's *Lehrlinge zu Sais,* which Gide had recently read. The voyage of the "Orion" is a dream adventure through
desire; an "invitation au voyage" of which the first condition is that
the pilgrims leave their pasts and their books behind. These young
men, wearied by fruitless studies, set out on an unpremeditated
journey. Yet they dimly understand their "valor" will be tested, and
vaguely long for heroism. The sirens are encountered early enough
in the voyage, and before the first month is out some of the sailors
have deserted. To go ashore and there be led astray is of course the
obvious temptation. But the obscure temptation to bathe beside the
ship or elsewhere soon seems more dangerous. The pilgrims who
remain on board, or who watch the others but abstain, eagerly
question them concerning the forbidden joys, until these others have
a right to say: "Here are bold chevaliers! Are you afraid even to taste
the fruit? And does your barren virtue consist only in abstinence and
doubt?" After the obvious sensuous enticements and pestilential
languors of "The Dolorous Ocean" comes the ennui of "The Sar-
gasso Sea": the ennui which follows not upon surfeit but upon the
annihilation of desire. Here the pilgrims casually encounter Ellis
(Urien's destined soul mate) or at least a woman who resembles her,
and the ship passes over a submerged city. The same day they observe
the first blocks of ice. A few, sick with ennui, must be left behind,
but the eight who remain embark on the "Voyage to a Glacial Sea."

The goal proves to be a disappointing, "apathetic," and unfrozen
little lake. The pilgrims wonder then whether it is perhaps better not
to attain one's goal, but decide that the joy of effort and satisfied
pride is reward enough. What then has been the voyage's and the
book's meaning? That it is impossible to achieve genuine peace without having led the will through evil, through the temptations of
passion and sluggish indifference? "The hard trials are past. Far
away are the gloomy shores where we thought we should die of

ennui; farther still the shores of illicit joys; let us count ourselves
fortunate to have experienced them. One cannot come here except
through them. To the loftiest cities lead the straightest ways: we are
going to the heavenly city." This statement, which may be attached
so easily to Gide's total meaning, comes at the beginning, not the end
of the "Voyage to a Glacial Sea," and is almost the only one to
offer such a comforting explicitness. It is perhaps better to avoid all
intellectual paraphrase; to admit that any ethical summary of *Le
Voyage d'Urien* falsifies the impression it makes.

For the adventures seem truly gratuitous, unless interpreted psychologically. And here precisely lies the historic interest of *Le
Voyage d'Urien,* which has never been fully recognized: it is a distinct and important episode in the transition from symbolism to surrealism; from the mysterious but somber soul-voyages of symbolism
to the free absurdity of surrealist nightmare. Some of the gratuity
reminds us vaguely of *The Ancient Mariner* and directly of *Arthur
Gordon Pym.* The mysterious ship of the dead which appears and
disappears could have been borrowed from either work, or borrowed simply from legend. Gide's Paride disintegrates as easily as
Poe's Peters, one losing an arm and the other a leg. Gide's Eskimo
community is more sophisticated and less cruel than Poe's; at a
crucial hour his pilgrims find a warning message written blazingly
on ice, as Poe's find a message in stone. Poe's water gets warmer as
we near the South Pole, and at Gide's North Pole we find an unfrozen lake. The mysterious sheep woman of *Le Voyage d'Urien*
recalls the numerous sheep lost in Maeterlinck's marshes, but also
the white luminous deity at the end of *Arthur Gordon Pym.* Most
interesting of all, in both works, is the gratuitous menace of water.
"I felt a numbness of body and mind," Poe's narrator tells us, "a
dreaminess of sensation. . . ." He watches an animal float by. "I
would have picked it up, but there came over me a sudden listless-
ness, and I forbore. The heat of the water still increased, and the
hand could no longer be endured within it. Peters spoke little, and
I knew not what to think of his apathy." [2]

It takes no psychiatric bias to see that *Arthur Gordon Pym* also
dramatizes preconscious longings and fears. There is nevertheless a
great difference between the two works, which brings Gide's much
closer to surrealism. Except in the final pages, Poe is as careful to

[2] These similarities are not offered as proof that Gide was influenced by *Arthur
Gordon Pym,* which he may or may not have read by 1892. They merely help
us to "locate" *Le Voyage d'Urien* in a general literary movement.

prepare and justify his mysteries as any Gothic novelist. Gide, on
the other hand, does not even bother to explain how his pilgrims
happened to set out. There is no logic in the connection of events,
other than an inner logic of psychological necessity. Streams may
flow backward; the *Orion* may "become" a felucca in an instant; a
monument—"for some unknown reason"—may suddenly rise out of
a plain. The mysterious child of the sixth chapter is perhaps borrowed from Novalis, but Ellis is borrowed from no one. The pilgrims' first meeting with her is a midpoint, as is were, between the
revery of Poe or Baudelaire and the dense inconsecutiveness of
Roussel's *Impressions d'Afrique*; the meeting is completely unprepared. We may even see the transition between the two modes, in
successive paragraphs. The first paragraph is in the symbolist manner, the second in the surrealist.

> The fourth day on the banks some smoke-colored herons hunted
> worms in the ooze; beyond them a level lawn extended. At night
> beneath reflected clouds pallid in the lingering day, the river appeared
> to run in a straight line, for the banks were hidden in shadow. The
> oars of the felucca, as they turned, caught in the reeds of the bank.

> The seventh day we met my dear Ellis, who was awaiting us on the
> lawn seated under an apple tree. She had been there a fortnight, hav-
> ing arrived before us by the overland route. She wore a polka-dot
> dress and carried a cerise parasol. Behind her was a little valise with
> toilet articles and some books; a Scotch shawl was over her arm; she
> was eating a salad of escarole and reading *The Prolegomena to All
> Future Metaphysics*. We had her climb into the boat.

It is difficult to argue the influence of *Le Voyage d'Urien* or of *Les
Chants de Maldoror,* alike unread at the time, against the influence
of Rimbaud and Laforgue. But in terms of Gide's own development,
the absurdity of the second part of *Le Voyage d'Urien* certainly led
to *Paludes, Le Prométhée mal enchaîné,* and *Les Caves du Vatican.*
And these, we know, had a real influence on surrealism.

The major interest of *Le Voyage d'Urien* is nevertheless a personal
and psychological interest. The "objective psychic content" would
be inviting under any circumstances: the transparently homosexual
reactions, the accumulated images of dissolution, the unexplained
fears of water and submersion in water.[3] This psychological interest

---

[3] Robert O'Clair, in my seminar on the modern novel, shrewdly observed that
"the great difficulty which one finds in trying to apply Rank and Freud to the
Voyage is that the narrative does not offer sufficient resistance to analysis."

becomes compelling—dangerously compelling—when we consider
the circumstances under which the book was written. It is the last of
Gide's books to precede his discovery of his homosexual nature, and
immediately preceded that discovery. It is therefore only too easy to
find—in the increasing homosexual language—a literal and dramatic
breaking of submerged forces to the troubled surface of consciousness. The danger is that we should infer too much about the creativ-
ity of the preconscious from this single instance, where many in-
stances would be needed for proof. But beyond this we know, from
Si le grain ne meurt, that *Le Voyage d'Urien* accompanied that same
struggle with masturbation which affected *André Walter*:

> At La Roque, the summer before the last, I thought I would go
> mad. There I spent nearly all my time cloistered in the room where
> only work should have kept me, trying in vain to work (I was then
> writing the *Voyage d'Urien*) . . . haunted and obsessed. Hoping per-
> haps to find some escape through excess itself, and to recover equa-
> nimity beyond it; hoping to debilitate my demon (I see there his
> advice) and debilitating only myself—I spent myself obsessively until
> exhausted; until there awaited me only imbecility and madness.

Given such a forthright statement, it would be amusing to demonstrate that the richer imagery and freer revery of *Le Voyage d'Urien*
were due to the fact that it was written during a period of excessive
self-indulgence, while *André Walter* was written during a period of
attempted self-control. But the fact that *André Walter* was a first
book, an exercise in learning to write, makes any such inference
dangerous. The biographical background of *Le Voyage d'Urien* is
unquestionably significant. But we will lose that significance if we
try to define it minutely.

"Souls are landscapes," says Gide's Preface to the second edition,
and the landscapes of *Le Voyage d'Urien* are fluid and dissolving.
Longing for fixity, the pilgrims travel past transforming shores
evanescent as "insincere actions." They explore floating islands, and
are lost among shifting dunes and moving knolls. Crossing an ambiguous plain they come upon a valley of mists, and then a prodigious
city of hanging gardens and fantastic minarets. But "the voices were
dying away; and as they fell, lo! the city faded, evanesced, disinte-
grated on a strophe; the minarets, the slender palms vanished; the
flights of stairs crumbled; sea and sand became visible through gardens on fading terraces." Some of the imagery of dissolution and pu-
trefaction must be discounted as symbolist and decadent commonplace. This is perhaps least true where the dissolving agent is water—

warm water, the recurrent menace on this voyage of the Puritan will.
In the queen's grotto air and diaphanous water merge, and solid
objects seem magically displaced. Icebergs melt in warm water at
significant moments in the story. Can we not see in the corpse, imprisoned in a solid ice wall, a wishful image of fixity and unmenaced
purity?

If we are to believe *Si le grain ne meurt*, Gide did not yet know
where the real menace lay. The homosexual images and reactions,
so curiously uncensored, must be accepted as undeliberate too. Like
Huxley's noble savage, Angaire fears that even the slightest tenderness will cause women to take off their clothes, and he admits preferring solitary pleasure. The pilgrims walk away from a performance
by whirling dervishes when their flowing robes become too revealing.
That evening the sailors bathe in the warm water and then lie down
on deck, "writhing with desire." But the pilgrims do not bathe, nor
do they dare even lie down. On another occasion the sailors return
from their sexual exploits, bringing fruits which bleed like wounds.
In Queen Haiatalnefus' realm the native men have long since re-
tired to live by themselves. There remain on the streets boys with
women's faces, or women with the faces of boys, "admirable creatures." And significantly enough, Ellis must dissolve before Urien
can unite either with her or with God.

In one remarkable chapter, we shall see, an almost uncensored
homosexual imagery supports the binding symbol of water. More
obvious and less interesting is the explicit disgust with normal sexual
experience—yet not entirely normal, since through one fevered night
the sailors and native women engaged in "incomplete embraces."
The equation could not be simpler: those who traffic with the
native women vomit, contract the plague, and die, while those who
abstain survive. The three crucial expeditions into narrow, sheltered
yet dangerous places suggest no such conscious meanings. The
queen's grotto is a lovely place, approached through calm canals
overhung by creepers and trees; the second grotto is a shadowed
place of stagnant waters, where lethargic bats hang from the ceiling.
The narrow fiord of the third part is "gloomy" and with somber
depths. The invitation is pressing to see in all three only the trauma
of birth—yet still more evident seems the imaged fear of normal
sexual penetration. The pilgrims find no difficulty leaving these narrow places but great difficulty entering them. In the first grotto they
refuse to bathe because of the crabs, sea nettles, and "cruel" lobsters.
Ellis contracts swamp fever in the second, and there first causes

Urien to doubt her identity. Auks nest on the cliffs of the fiord. Frightened, the females abandon their eggs, which roll down the rocks and shatter in "horrible streaks of white and yellow." Is there not some significance in the fact that Eric's wanton destructiveness, in hurling rocks at the birds, occurs at this particular point in the story?

The water, in any event, is "polluted" by the eggs—and we may want to take the actual consistencies of water into account when we consider the pilgrims' attitude toward bathing.[4] Only "water born of ice" seems wholly pure and invigorating. Yet the saffron-skinned men who bring snow from the icehouses of the original port have "bloody loincloths," and the blue water of the harbor is stained by bales of purple and dissolving dyes. Plague-stricken for their orgies, the sailors and native women "pollute" the water of the wash-houses with their "defiled tunics." "With long poles they stirred the slime at the bottom; clouds of sediment arose; bubbles came to the surface and burst. Bent over the rim, they inhaled these odors of the fen without revulsion; they laughed, for they were already stricken." The significance of these sentences derives from the fact that they are wholly gratuitous.

Water is yet the attractive as it is the destructive element, and the temptation to bathe is a more real one than any encountered on land. On the fifth day the pilgrims swim in the ocean and are penetrated by the "languor" of the waves. Later they refuse to bathe out of fear of the sirens whom their less courageous shipmates have visited. On a third occasion the sailors, bathing after sexual indulgence, are beautiful yet "gleam with unwonted pallor." A single sentence concludes the sixth chapter: "We did not bathe that day." The effect "is of a statement in code"—and the obvious inference is that bathing is simply equated with sexual indulgence, which is both ruinous and beautiful. A full census of the baths taken by pilgrims and sailors supports this equation, which may even have been an intentional one. Tepid water is the property which debilitates, which dissolves will and energy. But it is also the obscure source of riches and dreams. The longing to bathe may also be a

[4] For an interesting psychoanalytic interpretation of water pollution, see Gaston Bachelard, *L'Eau et les rêves* (Paris, 1942), chapter vi. Water is the image of the mother, as the sun of the father; pure water is—for the unconscious —an appeal to pollution. The four volumes of Bachelard's *Essai sur l'imagination de la matière* reveal a wide literary culture and a sensitive critical talent; all four volumes should be translated.

longing to dissolve the personality, to rejoin the healing depths of
the unconscious, to achieve Jungian integration. When Queen
Haiatalnefus drops one of her rings into the sea, Urien refuses to
join the other pilgrims in diving after it—"not through ennui, but
on the contrary through a desire too great, so fascinated had I always been by the mysterious depths of the waves." His companions
remain long under water, and on their return fall into a deep sleep.
"A numbing torpor at first drugged my senses," Clarion says on
awaking, "and I thought only of the pure slumber I could have in
that cool water, couched on the soft seaweed." [5] Later, the submarine
city beneath their ship is an azured vision of repose; it fills Urien
with a "lyric ecstasy." In unconsciousness and in death, in water, the
miserable self may be dissolved.

The desire to dissolve the self thus seems to take on several forms
in *Le Voyage d'Urien,* and to have a multiple meaning. A verbalized
and conscious longing for fixity is affronted by the spectacle of a dissolving universe. But what does this longing for fixity really signify,
and does it not cover a less conscious longing to be one of the dissolving forms? And what would dissolution itself bring, if accomplished
in these tepid waters: escape from the "miserable personality," or
the riches of restored energy, or sexual release and expense? A
passage from the *Lehrlinge zu Sais* suggests that these impulses may
be, at a given moment, inextricably connected: "He felt his miserable
personality melt, submerged beneath waves of pleasure, and that
nothing remained but a home for the incommensurable genetic force
—a whirlpool in which everything is swallowed by the vast ocean.
What does the flame ubiquitously offer? An intimate embrace, from
which the sweet liquid trickles in voluptuous drops." [6]

---

[5] For Jung, Clarion would have descended to the collective unconscious (and
hence achieved "the restoration of life, the resurrection, and the conquest of
death"); and in the same act would have successfully dissolved personality and
lost his burdensome identity. "It is the world of water, where everything floats
in suspension; where the kingdom of the sympathetic system, of the soul of
everything living, begins; where *I* am inseparably this and that, and this and
that are I; where I experience the other person in myself, and the other, as myself, experiences me" (*The Integration of the Personality,* translated by Stanley
Dell [New York, 1939], pp. 242, 70).

[6] This reminder of the *Lehrlinge zu Sais* (which Gide had read, and which
he virtually paraphrased on one page of *Le Voyage d'Urien*) raises an old
but important question. In weighing the psychological significance of a text, how
much must we discount as mere literary imitation? Certainly Novalis treated
more consciously than the Gide of 1892 both *Auflösung* (the dissolution of the
soul in nature) and *Einfühlung* (the projection of the self into nature). *Le*

Compared with the diffuse *Lehrlinge zu Sais, Le Voyage d'Urien*
has the density and economy of the most conscious art. Yet the fifth
chapter of the first part—which conveys both the latent homosexuality and the fear of dissolution—must certainly have escaped any
rational "intention" and all but the most rudimentary of unconscious censorship. It forces upon us not merely the equivalence of
water, indulgence and dissolution, but also the very physical terms
of the homosexual embrace. The pilgrims go to a coral islet, and
there watch fishermen dive for coral, sponges, and pearls. "The men
had saffron-colored skin; they were naked, but around their necks
hung bags to be filled with shells." They must cut away with knives
the tentacles which attach to their bodies; when they come to the
surface their lungs contract, and a thread of blood—"sumptuous on
their golden skin"—almost makes them faint. The pilgrims are "di-
verted" by seeing the ocean floor and the blood of these men. They
then bathe themselves in pools which are too warm and in which
children are playing. At the bottom of a pool are mosaic figures and
two statues that spout perfume into basins. The pilgrims allow the
perfume to flow over their arms and hips. And soon a torpor comes
over them, as they breathe "this tepid mist—immobile, floating,
abandoned; in vain swooning in the marvelous water, green and
blue, where glowed only the dimmest light, where the arms of the

---

Voyage d'Urien seems, on the other hand, a much less metaphysical and a much
more personal document. It is reasonable to suppose that Novalis' novel may
have suggested the frame of a pilgrimage to the divine city ("every new road
traverses new countries, and leads us at last to these dwellings we dream of, to
the sacred homeland"), and that his turbulent images of dissolution may have
encouraged in Gide an already existing area of feeling. Beyond this it would
be unwise to go. A much more obvious "source" is Maeterlinck's *Serres Chaudes*
(1891). Some two-thirds of the poems deal with lassitude and ennui, and six-
teen out of thirty-three have hospitals or gratuitously sick people. "Cloche à
plongeur" in particular may have suggested much to Gide. We find, in thirty-
three Whitmanesque lines, a gulf-stream specifically linked with "ennui"; ice-
ships; whales encountered on the way to the pole; snow applied to the foreheads
of the fevered; obscure grottos; flames on the sea; sailing-ships passing over
submarine forests. A few sentences are still more suggestive: "Ils arrivent comme
des vierges qui ont fait une longue promenade au soleil, un jour de jeûne
. . . Et fermez bien vos yeux en restant sourd aux suggestions de l'eau tiède
. . . Et tout attouchement à jamais interdit!" It seems undeniable that Gide
"echoed" Maeterlinck. But what does this prove? Perhaps no more than that
we may arrive at highly personalized imagery—the imagery which expresses our
most intimate conflicts—through the reading of innocent texts. No one would
argue, I think, after a comparison with *Le Voyage d'Urien*, that "Cloche à
plongeur" is more than a "literary" or "innocent" text.

slender children were tinted blue by the light, and drops falling from
the ceiling plashed in monotone." That evening the sailors and the
weaker of the pilgrims go on shore in search of women, and those
who remain on board are tormented by the thought of their embraces. There is an enormous red moon; there are fires on shore; the
night is unbearably hot over the phosphorescent sea. And now we
learn, abruptly, that the pilgrims have been watching the sleeping
fishermen: "And out of the forest wide-winged vampires, prowling
near the sleeping fishermen, sucked the life from their naked feet,
from their lips, and overwhelmed them with slumber by the silent
beating of their wings."

All this is conveyed in a little more than five hundred words. It
should be emphasized that there are no logical connections between
the four "episodes": the observation of the fishermen, the swim in
the magic pool and subsequent torpor, the evening restlessness on
the ship, the coming of the vampires. There are no transitional
phrases, yet not a single word breaks the prevailing and complex
mood. Mere revery—which normally results in such diffuseness—has
here imposed rather than destroyed unity by the very urgency of its
demand: by its longing for a nevertheless dreaded relaxation, by its
"selection" of particular and revealing imagery. However florid some
of its pages, *Le Voyage d'Urien* already shows Gide's ability to record
feelings exactly; to penetrate—more successfully than he knew—
beneath the level of full consciousness.

The *Récits*

by *Jean Hytier*

That Gide is a novelist is contestable. We shall have to decide the question apropos of *Les Faux-Monnayeurs*. Yet he is universally recognized as a master of the *récit*. *L'Immoraliste, La Porte étroite, Isabelle, La Symphonie pastorale* are four authentic masterpieces which enrich that magnificent tradition of French literature which includes *la Princesse de Clèves, Manon Lescaut, René, Adolphe, Carmen, Dominique. . . .*

These *récits* have often been misunderstood, primarily because they have been taken for more or less fictionalized confessions, secondly because they have been read without being "placed" in the ensemble of Gide's works, and finally because their hidden irony has not been discerned. Gide explicitly states in one of his *Feuillets:*

> With the single exception of my *Nourritures,* all my books are *ironic* works; *they are books of criticism. La Porte étroite* is the criticism of a certain form of romantic imagination; *La Symphonie pastorale,* of a form of lying to oneself; *L'Immoraliste,* of a form of individualism.

The *récits* therefore constitute a part of the same series of tendentious works to which the *soties* belonged. They too are satires, although Gide has hedged a bit here (" 'Criticism' doesn't mean the same thing as 'satire' "), but of a special nature: they are serious and indirect satires. We all know that a portrait painted with great fidelity and complete submission to the model can be infinitely more cruel than caricature, especially since, being truthful, it leaves no margin for the illusion of a systematic distortion against which the model could protest. Gide's *récits* are like those implacable portraits in which the painter's very love for his subject serves only to

" The *Récits*." From Jean Hytier, *André Gide,* trans. Richard Howard, pp. 120–47. Originally published by Editions Charlot, Paris, 1938. Reprinted by permission of Doubleday & Co., Inc., Constable & Co., Ltd., and Jean Hytier.

reinforce—emotionally—the severity of his vision by a deliberate accuracy.

What further differentiates the *récits* from the *soties* is the role of irony. Whereas *Paludes* and the *Prométhée* are steeped in it, and though it circulates freely in *Les Caves du Vatican,* aiming even at Lafcadio in places (though rarely; this character, merely grazed by it, is in fact treated in the manner of the heroes of the *récits,* whom irony illuminates but does not overpower), there is no direct attack in the *récits.* The characters the narrator encounters may well be ridiculed by him, but only from his own point of view, not that of the author, who stubbornly remains in the wings. It is in order to attain a higher degree of objectivity that Gide has handed his pen to the four characters who tell these stories, and whose nature must indeed be ignored in order to mistake them for him; any comparison eloquently testifies to this separateness: a fierce individualist (the hero of *L'Immoraliste*); a fervent Protestant, amorous and yet apathetic (Jérôme in *La Porte étroite*); a sentimental university student who dreams of being a novelist (Gérard Lacase in *Isabelle*); a Swiss pastor who confuses the voice of conscience and the voice of instinct (the minister in *La Symphonie pastorale*). One certainly divines, or is expressly told in the *Journal* and in *Si le grain ne meurt . . . ,* what Gide's personal experience may have contributed to the life of these beings, and with what supple skill he has wisely made them speak in the first person; we see how well he could mimic himself, but each time by exploring only a part of himself, driving himself to absurd extremes—Gide, who always wanted to be at the *extrême milieu,* who always dreamed of equilibrium and proportion, whom Claudel defined as "a mind without propensity." Still we must make this reservation, that Gide's sympathy, his interest in others, permits him an objective mimetism that produces the pastor who tells *La Symphonie pastorale* and whom he nonetheless opposed from the bottom of his heart. Gide's mastery seems to me to consist precisely in utilizing all his powers of sympathy and antipathy; by sympathy, he makes these *first persons singular* speak with an accent of truth unequaled in French fiction, and the author's *I* realizes possibilities far beyond the *I* of Gide the man; by antipathy, he maintains all his reserve, marks the distances which separate him from his creatures, and keeps a margin of irony between the frame and the drawing of these figures, executed with a mixture of attachment and detachment that is classical in its sureness.

The surface interest of these *récits* has obscured their critical aspect; readers let themselves be carried away, and react naïvely to the story they are being told, and this is indeed part of Gide's intentions; but he also intends the reader to withdraw his identification, either by the story's end or, perhaps still more, as it is being told.

The extension of the adventures of these singular spirits in the reader's mind, and the accompaniment to them, is a critical reflection which detaches him from them and keeps him from granting a predominant, excessive importance to the total emotion he may be tempted to derive from them. If the immoralist Michel horrifies him, if Alissa pierces his heart with pity, if Isabelle disillusions him, if the pastor irritates him, he must not allow his feelings for the fate of these heroes to turn against their author; instead he will praise Gide for having been able to provoke with such intensity a response that attests to the artist's sureness of touch and powers of evocation. He will avoid the naïveté of asserting his own feelings as a reproach to Gide's. For Gide is horrified by his "superman"; he admires Alissa and is distressed by her demanding virtue; Jérôme's apathy seems ruinous to him; he despises the seductive Isabelle and ridicules Gérard's over-obliging imagination; he is irritated by the pastor's unconscious hypocrisy. In fact the irony begins only after a perfect comprehension of these beings, and for Gide, no doubt, of himself. The irony consists in not accepting them, however human or superhuman they may be, and however touched we are by their motives or their condition, by value or virtue, by sanctity itself. We must, however much it goes against the grain, reject them. They are dangerous examples. The Gidean irony lies in this transcendence, which always costs us something, for there is a kind of horrible courage in Michel, an exalting appeal in Alissa's renunciations, a pictistic respect in Jérôme's inaction, a charm in Gérard's romanticism, an intoxicating seductiveness in the portrait of the unreal Isabelle, an evangelistic fervor and kindness in the pastor. It is a heroic irony. Hence the deep resonance of these unforgettable works, even after we have plumbed their secret. Rereading them, we always fall under their spell again.

And yet Gide has seemingly wished to keep us at a distance. His advice is always not to follow whatever path he has shown us: "Nathanaël, throw away my book." The irony of these works is curiously placed. In *L'Immoraliste* it is in the conclusion that the reader will draw from it, the relentless story not having left him time to collect himself before Marceline's dreadful death march and the exhaustion of the hero's inhuman tendency. In *La Porte étroite,* Jérôme's respectful inaction wakens a muted irony at each of his self-effacements, but the last lines of the *Journal d'Alissa* burn with a despairing irony at the notion of her anguish when she divines the total futility of her ascent toward virtue and her solitude achieved without God. More muted, the irony of *Isabelle* is in the movement that erodes our mysterious enchantment; it accompanies the decrescendo of the fictional illusion, the wretched collapse of an imaginary charm. In *La Symphonie pastorale,* as in a comedy, the irony lies in the gap between the pastor's naïve words and the unacknowledged feelings they conceal, between his conscience and his unconscious; it makes him the reader's pathetic plaything.

If this irony, sometimes muted, sometimes lightly etched upon the story's transparency, sometimes concealed in an intention that exceeds it, yields the secret of each of these *récits,* none gives us Gide's whole thought. To arrive at this, we must complete them by each other; and it is obvious, for example, that the excesses of egoism in *L'Immoraliste* and of sacrifice in *La Porte étroite* counterbalance one another; but for a total view, we must actually take all of Gide's work into account, oppose the impotent exasperation of *Paludes* to the harsh energy of *L'Immoraliste,* the parody of sanctity in the *Prométhée* to the sublimity of *La Porte étroite,* the destructiveness of *Saül* to the enrichment of *Les Nourritures,* the altruism of *Le Roi Candaule* to the egoism of *L'Immoraliste, etc.* . . . The most cursory indication of these necessary comparisons suggests that Gide's entire work is a kind of symphony whose significance is not in this or that part, but in their harmony, their unison, and by this I mean their contrast as much as their concert. There are only two books in which Gide has tried to put all of himself—prematurely, in *André Walter*; at the peak of his maturity, in *Les Faux-Monnayeurs.* We understand why Gide has reserved for this last book alone the designation *novel:* a novel worthy of the name must, in effect, communicate a whole world, represent an author's entire vision, orchestrate all the parts of his imagination. In a sense, the total of Gide's *récits* and *soties* would be the substance of a vast novel integrating them in a varied unity. *Les Caves du Vatican* might be said to afford something like a rough draft of this polyphony, with the contrasts of its double plot, the variety of its characters, their varied situations in society, but in tone and intention it is not so much a novel as a parody of a novel, the comedy of the novel—moreover, one admirably executed. And here again Gide has contrived a relation with another of his works: *Les Faux-Monnayeurs* corresponds, on the serious level, to

this farcical work. Moreover we know that in an initial plan, Lafcadio was to be the narrator of *Les Faux-Monnayeurs* and enter into
relations with the novelist Edouard; Gide was certainly right to cut
the links that united the two conceptions and to set apart, at the
summit of his work, this great attempt to objectify his entire inner
world. I shall study this work later, and if I refer to it here, it is
because it allows us to see more clearly the nature of these *récits*
without which Gide could doubtless not later have conceived and
mastered such a network of intersecting intentions. Each of the
récits is in fact remarkable for the purity of its line, the elegant
singleness of its contour, the sobriety of its development and, for
once to use this word in praise, its *unilaterality*.

I think that what distinguishes the tale from the novel is its minimum of intricacy, its continuous *melody*. Without proliferating incident or episode, Gide has admirably understood the technical purity
this genre requires, as opposed to the novel, where only proliferation
and interconnection can give the impression of total life. In the tale,
one takes a sounding which of course respects divagations but must
especially preserve, in its elegant abstraction, the separateness of its
singular object. At the core of *L'Immoraliste,* of *La Porte étroite,* of
Isabelle, of *La Symphonie pastorale,* we find a simple *donnée,* a single germ; and Gide's art has been precisely to bring this seed into
flower, not forcing it, but encouraging its bloom with the patience
and the love of a good gardener. One human being who prefers
himself to everything and sacrifices everything to himself, another
who prefers everything to herself and sacrifices herself totally; the
disillusionment of an overweening imagination, the blinding of
desire by the lies of conscience—such subjects sufficed to give these
tales the *élan* of classical perfection.

The art of the novel tends to create in the reader emotional states
which approach those of poetry. In French this tendency is called, in
fact, *le romanesque*. It would not be difficult to show that Gide's
récits achieve powerful effects and that, on this point, he is a match
for the most spellbinding storytellers. We need merely to recall our
horrified admiration for the immoralist's criminal madness, the hideous impression of Marceline's death, the anguished and despairing
sublimity to which we are swept by the ascetic renunciation of
Alissa's mysticism, the contemptuous melancholy on which *romanesque* illusion is wrecked in *Isabelle,* the outraged pity the blind
girl's suicide wakens in us, the culmination of the self-duped pastor's

folly. The whole range of feelings, from the most powerful to the most subtly tinted, is explored by Gide. It is difficult to surpass the pathos of Alissa's growing solitude.

We realize how readily the novel may contain all genres: tragedy, comedy, poetry. And the tale can, precisely, isolate—whereas the novel must mingle—any one of these great fundamental emotions which are at the core of the ensemble effects by which the genres may be distinguished. From this point of view, then, these four *récits* of Gide's are tragedies: they are all determined by deaths, save one, *Isabelle* (not counting the deaths of the minor characters), which ends in a collapse of the heroine that is worse than death. As a bloodless tragedy, all things considered, it is Gide's *Bérénice*. And apparent in all of them, more than the *romanesque,* is a profound poetry consisting of our distressed sympathy for all these splendid themes of true suffering, for all these excesses of unchecked vitality, of elevation to the absolute, of the romanticizing of reality, of mortal hypocrisy. It is against this poetry—abjured yet so deeply felt—that resolute irony gains a footing, not without regrets, not without bitterness.

But if the novel borders on poetry by these affective fulfillments even as it approaches the drama by the creation of characters and the imposition of their destiny, it seems to me that the true pleasure proper to the novel is to achieve an original vision of the world by the invention of a fictional universe which does not duplicate the one we live in but takes its inspiration from it in order to recreate it, or rather to reinterpret it and thereby give us a new explanation of it, astonishing, if not shocking. I therefore propose to define the novel as a metaphysic of the intelligence, regarding that pleasure proper to it as an intellectual pleasure. We shall return more forcefully to this conception apropos of *Les Faux-Monnayeurs,* but it is necessary to suggest it here with regard to Gide's tales. For even an author of tales who never writes a true novel, one rivaling life itself in complexity, has his metaphysic nonetheless: he merely disperses it in fragmentary aspects (like Mérimée, like Maupassant) instead of centering and organizing it in huge ensembles (like Balzac, like Dostoevsky). To grasp this metaphysic in the author of tales, we must gather up and compare in an ideal gallery these separate portraits of a world even more his own than that of reality. And though Gide has given us his total vision in *Les Faux-Monnayeurs,* the four *récits* we are considering here do not fail to present certain common characteristics. All are narratives of *disappointment.* All touch us, distress and irritate us; but intellectually they show us characters imprisoned in a formula, captives of a rule, a law, a convention or a habit, and victims of themselves. They have all *chosen* and have found themselves prisoners of a choice—of a choice whose distinguishing mode is, respectively, harshness, narrowness, facility, or deception. The reader will recognize once again the horror of choice, a sign in Gide of rigidity and ossification in an attitude, a sign of thralldom, of impoverishment, and no doubt of imbecility, of weakness, of deficiency, whether its source is the absolutism of desire, the exaltation of virtue, the seduction of the imagination, or the complacencies of conscience. The fraudulence of his goal imprisons man in a fatality. If these tragic works are cruelly crowned by irony, it is because for Gide intelligence is an essential value; it is because the critical spirit is at the basis of all true progress and, no doubt, of all true love as well. That even the critical spirit is liable to distortions, Lafcadio has shown us. One might follow it at work in everything Gide writes, notably in his plays and above all in *Les Faux-Monnayeurs,* where I am tempted to see it, more than the devil in whom Gide has not succeeded in making us believe, as the true protagonist.

The work of a novelist or a storyteller might theoretically be regarded as the result of an impulse to analyze and an impulse to synthesize. Out of reality, which he starts from and which comprehends his inner life as well as the spectacle of the outer world, his imagination abstracts elements which interest it and to which it accords a new place, role and value in an original recomposition, guided by his intellectual metaphysic. The error of certain novelists is to confine themselves to analysis. Every work of art is synthetic and organic. Consequently each novelist, each storyteller has his own way of resolving the problem of the relations of reality and imagination. Gide's method may be expressed in two words: *development* of possibilities, and *transposition.*

In the web of events and characters which forms the basis of the *récit,* Gide does not start with actions or circumstances, he starts with the actors; more precisely, he starts with a complex of feelings which has moved him, and whose communicative warmth he wishes to restore. He has explained himself on this matter in *Un esprit non prévenu.* There are, he says, two ways of depicting life.

The one, external and commonly called "objective," first sees the gestures of other men, the event, and then explains and interprets them.

The other, which is primarily attached to the emotions, to thoughts, invents incidents and characters most suitable to express these emotions—and risks remaining incapable of painting anything which has not first been experienced by the author. The latter's resources, his complexities, the antagonism of his too-diverse possibilities, will permit the greatest diversity among his creations. But it is from him that everything emanates. He is the sole guarantee of the truth he reveals, and the sole judge. The heaven and hell of his characters are in him. It is not himself that he paints; but what he paints he might have become had he not become everything himself.

It is, then, a personal method, one which claims to draw everything from the self. But it does not proceed by a naïve expression of the novelist's dreams; it proceeds by abstraction, isolating a tendency and causing it to fructify by yielding to its impulse.

How many buds we bear within us . . . which never flower in our books! They are "sleeping eyes," as the botanists call them. But if, out of determination, we get rid of them all, save one, how it grows then, how it swells! how quickly it monopolizes the sap! To create a hero, my recipe is a simple one: Take one of these buds, put it in a pot—all alone—and an admirable specimen soon results. A word of advice: preferably select (if it is true that you have a choice) the bud that bothers you most. You get rid of it at the same time. This may be what Aristotle called the purgation of the passions.

In this way Michel, Alissa, and the pastor represent not Gide, but possibilities of his soul, and are authentically his creatures. The mistake begins when one claims to limit Gide to them. In their author's real life, these characters have never been tolerated; they have been opposed to each other and balanced:

That there is a bud of Michel in me goes without saying; but this is a case of those opposing passions Pascal describes so cleverly, which maintain themselves in equilibrium because we cannot yield to one save to the other's detriment.

To reduce Gide to one of his characters is to diminish him wrongly. "If I were only the hero (I don't say: the author) of *L'Immoraliste* . . . I should feel myself diminished."

As a matter of fact, Gide possesses a second method, for he has not modeled quite all his characters on himself. There are doubtless some whose germ was not within him. Nothing could be further from his nature than Jérôme's apathy or Marceline's weakness. But

this second method, a complement of the first, eventually unites
with it, in an odd way. For to abandon yourself in imagination to
one of your tendencies, submitting to its demands, is not far, in
practice, from the converse operation, which consists in borrowing
from the external world a disposition which is alien to you and
lending yourself to it with such force of sympathy that little by little
it seems to become natural to you, and personal. In the first case
Gide encourages the budding; in the second, he performs a graft,
and perhaps I admire the artist in the second instance even more.
In both, submissive attention replaces an active *parti pris*. The
flowering is observed with the same patience. But if Gide has perhaps not clearly distinguished these two operations on account of
the equivalent sympathy they require (whether for a part of oneself
or for another person's tendency), nothing better suggests how
greatly they are opposed in origin than this curious passage where
the mimetism of the external world is resolved in the disappearance
of the self:

> Nothing is accomplished if I have not been truly able to become
> this character I am creating, and to depersonalize myself in him until
> I put my readers on the wrong scent and risk incurring the reproach
> of never being able to paint any portrait but my own, however dif-
> ferent Saül, Candaule, Alissa, Lafcadio, the pastor of my *Symphonie,*
> La Pérouse, or Armand may be among themselves. It is returning to
> myself that embarrasses me; for to tell the truth, I no longer know who
> I am; or, if your prefer: I never am, I become.

No doubt there are also cases—this would be a third kind—where
the invasion of the self by a borrowed nature is based on a scission
of the personality, in one part of which it finds an echo: this, I
presume, would be the typical case of Alissa, whose heroic nature
has found an analogy in Gide's early mysticism. But Gide has not
taken all of Alissa from himself. He has received a suggestion from
the real world and reinforced it by his personal fervor (or the
memory of that fervor).

It would be an oversimplification not to take into account the fact
that Gide must also have struggled against too complete an abnegation of himself. The latter, in certain cases, would have resulted in
a stalemate. Becoming once again as mystical as his pastor, he would
have failed to make us aware of the deceptions of his conscience;
he would have adhered to his duplicity instead of showing it to us.
It is not surprising that this subtle stratagem awakened his impatience during the writing of *La Symphonie pastorale*: "Suddenly I

want to regain a state of fervor, and I am reluctant to let myself be
caught in it: I pull on the reins and use the whip at the same
time. . . ."

How different Gide can be, actually, from what he has most tried
to resemble is shown best in his skill at detaching himself from all
his heroes and judging them at a great distance from himself:

> No, I don't think Michel will ever write. His warmth, as you can
> tell, is only ardor; it burns without giving heat; the words would
> disintegrate under his pen. Believe me . . . it is only because I am
> not Michel that I could tell his story "so remarkably well," as you say.

And it is here, as the end of this passage proves, that the development of possibilities, of virtuality, is linked in Gide to *transposition.*
Actually his art lies in that miracle which reconciles attachment and
detachment. These are actually a painter's properties. Love and
criticism are here marvelously united to produce that combination
of warmth and impartiality which gives Gide's *récits* that extraordinary power of personal life and of serene objectivity. We can walk
around these characters, as around real persons. The sense of life
is not communicated, as in other great creators, by a kind of blood
transfusion brutally forced upon us, or by the warmth of an insolent
or embarrassing contact, but by the animation of independent creatures whose umbilical cord has been carefully cut.

"Only what has ceased to serve is suited to become the substance
of art." Gide here reveals one of his secrets. By memory, he recovers
the warmth necessary to the life of his heroes. By the detachment
of the past, he achieves the *sang-froid* which assures his technique
and keeps his hand from trembling. The more ardent the original
experience has been, and the more complete his liberation from it,
the better the work unites the domination of a faultless art with
the palpitation of recovered life. There is in Gide an incomparable
clarity in this separation of sentiment and intelligence, of the romanticism of passion and the classicism of expression. It is Gide who
defines true classicism as *romanticism mastered.* This desire to purify
substance is already quite apparent in the earliest and most intransigent of his *récits, L'Immoraliste:* "I spent four years not writing
but living it; and I wrote it to transcend it; I have had this book the
way you have a sickness. . . . I no longer admire any books save
those the author has only barely managed to survive." It is the
work in which he has succeeded least, moreover, in achieving that
sovereign domination of the object and which, from this point of
view, contains a certain technical impurity. There linger in it too

many "tatters of himself." Later, he will "absent himself" from his
récits. The temptation had been too strong, the fever too violent
(this cure is indeed the crucial phase of Gide's life); but if we sense
a certain effort in the admirable *domestication* of the powers of
anarchy from which the book is born, we must not presume that
elsewhere Gide has required any such strife. He knows that flexi-
bility, even cunning, is often the condition of an artistic success
which severity or harshness would destroy. It is with the greatest ease
that the *Journal d'Alissa* and her letters were composed: "how easy
it is for me," he says, "how voluptuous to yield to a being less complicated than myself and who, by that very fact, expresses herself
with less difficulty."

We need only compare Gide's confidences as to the circumstances
which inspired these *récits* with the use he has made of them to see
how far he is from naturalistic methods, from the documentary
techniques of the slice-of-life school. Nor is there anything in him
of the visionary, of Balzac's overblown amplification or Zola's epic
overexcitement. He enlarges no more than he reproduces. One
scarcely dares say that he transforms. He *transposes*. He brings to
another plane certain selected elements, following their secret or
significant directions, and not their picturesque or exotic details.
This is as true of his landscapes as of his characters. We know from
Si le grain ne meurt . . . that Anna Shackleton's death had first
suggested a *récit* which was to be called *Essai de bien mourir*. But
he effected another transposition:

"I was extremely affected by the thought that neither my mother
nor myself had been able to be with her at her last hour, that she
had not said goodbye to us and that her last glances had met only
strangers' eyes. For weeks and months I was filled with the anguish
of her solitude. I imagined, I even heard the desperate call and
then the collapse of this loving soul deserted by everything save
God; and it is the echo of this call that reverberates in the last pages
of my *Porte étroite*."

Alissa's Journal, October 15

Joy, joy, tears of joy. . . .
Exceeding human joy and beyond all pain, yes, I foresee this radiant
joy. This rock I cannot surmount, I know it has a name: happiness.
. . . I understand that all my life is in vain if I do not attain happiness. . . . Ah! yet, you promise it, Lord, to the soul that renounces
and is pure. "Blessed now," says your holy word, "blessed henceforth
are those who die in the Lord." Must I wait until death? It is here

that my faith stumbles, Lord! I cry out to you with all my strength.
I am in darkness; I wait for the dawn. I cry out to you until I die.
Come and slake my heart. I thirst for that happiness. . . . Or must
I persuade myself I have it now? And like the impatient cock that
crows before the dawn, summoning not announcing the day, must I
not wait for the night to pale before I sing?

October 16

Jérôme, I would teach you perfect joy.

This morning, a fit of vomiting weakened me terribly. Once it was
over, I felt so weak that for an instant I almost hoped for death.
But no; first a great calm came over my whole being; then an anguish
seized me, a shudder of the flesh and the spirit; it was like the sudden,
disenchanted illumination of my life. It seemed to me that for the
first time I saw the hideously bare walls of my room. I grew afraid.
Even now I am writing to reassure myself, to calm myself. O Lord! If
only I could have gone to the end without blasphemy.

I could still get up. I fell on my knees like a child. . . .

I would like to die now, quickly, before having understood again
that I am alone.

In the second part of *L'Immoraliste,* the Caux landscape has not
tempted Gide to a description *à la* Flaubert; his interpretation transforms its role from that of décor to a more affective existence: "It
is this valley which I have painted, and it is our house, in *L'Immoraliste.* The countryside has not only lent me its setting; throughout
the book, I have sought its likeness."

Just as he abstracts in order to encourage the flowering of a particularity of his nature, or as he grafts an alien sensibility onto himself in order to develop it, with the same freedom Gide detaches
from the chaos of experience some combination of circumstances,
some anecdote even, some natural setting or episodic figure, provided he finds significance and promise in it, and he preserves their
profound meaning by contriving a liberation which renders them
more faithful to themselves, so to speak, than they were in the
confusion and compromise from which he drew them. This double
sense of what must be necessarily arbitrary in art and of its inner
deepening has entirely freed Gide's *récits* from the vulgarity of the
naturalistic tradition and from the banality of facile psychologizing.

Sympathy and transposition were, moreover, obvious resources for
a storyteller like Gide who has not a great deal of imagination and
who refuses to transcribe nature literally. We have seen how his
subjects grew from the germination of an inner tendency. None-

theless the subject of *Isabelle* is borrowed from reality, as well as the setting, which is furnished by the estate of Formentin, near La Roque, Gide's property; most of the characters actually existed. The other *récits*, moreover, are laid in countries with which Gide was familiar: North Africa, Italy, Normandy (La Roque-Baignard in *L'Immoraliste*, and Cuverville-en-Caux in *La Porte étroite*), and last of all the Swiss Jura: it is at La Brévine that the action of *La Symphonie pastorale* is situated; *Paludes* had been written there, and Gide retained an unpleasant memory of a hostile population. When the social milieu is significant, Gide paints it with the same concern for likeness as his heroes, the same sobriety of means, the same power of hidden suggestion. Landscapes or interiors are inseparable from the beings who inhabit them. We can no longer think of Jérôme and Alissa without seeing the garden of their childhood and the little kitchen-garden gate; of Michel without imagining the apartment surrounded by terraces in the Biskra hotel.

In *Isabelle* the atmosphere plays the leading role. It is created not only by the old estate, its huge grounds, its old house and the summer house where Gérard finds the telltale letter, but just as much by the faded *bizarrerie* of the beings who inhabit La Quart-fourche. Here the characters create the décor, so strange do they seem. Recall the Floche household, and above all the Saint-Auréol couple, who in a museum "would immediately be classified among the extinct species," and whom Gide has described with a brief and picturesque humor that recalls the Chateaubriand of the *Mémoires d'outre-tombe*. *Isabelle* is distinguished by this *sotie* aspect. Emotion in it is less serious than in the other *récits*, because the supposed narrator is not deeply committed. *The Pathetic Illusion* (this was Gide's first title) is not deadly, like Alissa's utterly futile heroism; the dissolution of the *romanesque* is endurable and could not lead to suicide, like the despair of the blind girl who recovers her sight in *La Symphonie pastorale*. It is an ambiguous charm that imbues this "half-playful interlude between two over-serious works." The erotic reverie which nourishes the *romanesque* interest and the narrator's passionate curiosity is plunged into a milieu of a burlesque unreality where everything seems to grimace.

Isabelle has come by night, in secret, as is her custom, to seek help from her aunt:

> Madame Floche, poor old thing, was still holding her bunch of keys in one hand and in the other the meagre little bundle of notes she had taken out of the drawer; she was just going to seat herself again

in her arm-chair, when the door opposite that at which I was posted
was suddenly flung open—and I could hardly restrain a cry of stupefaction. The Baronne was standing stiffly in the doorway, décolleté,
rouged, in full ceremonial attire and her head surmounted by what
looked like a gigantic feather brush of marabout. She was staggering
under the weight of a great six-branched candelabra in which all the
candles were burning, flooding her with their flickering light and shed-
ding tears of wax all over the floor. She had come, no doubt, to the
end of her strength, for she began by hastily making for the table
and setting down the candelabra in front of the looking-glass; then,
taking four skips back to her position in the doorway, she once more
advanced, solemnly and with measured steps, stretching out at full
length in front of her a hand loaded with enormous rings. In the
middle of the room, she stood still, turned stiffly towards her daughter
and, with hand still outstretched, shrieked in ear-splitting accents:

"Get thee behind me, ungrateful daughter! Your tears can no longer
move me and your protestations have for ever lost the way to my
heart."

The whole speech was delivered with no variation of tone at the
topmost pitch of her voice. In the meantime, Isabelle had thrown
herself at her mother's feet and taken hold of her dress; as she pulled
it to one side, revealing two absurd little white satin slippers, she
herself continued to strike her forehead on the floor, where a rug was
spread over the boards. Madame de Saint-Auréol did not lower her
eyes for an instant; still looking straight before her, with glances as
piercing and icy as her voice, she continued:

"It is not enough for you to have brought poverty into the dwelling
of your parents? Are you contemplating a further . . ."

Here her voice suddenly failed her and she turned towards Madame
Floche who, making herself as small as she could, sat trembling in
her arm-chair:

"And as for you, Sister, if you are still so weak . . ." (she took herself up) "if you are still so unpardonably weak as to yield to her entreaties, even for one kiss—even for one groat—so true as I am your
elder sister, I leave you—I recommend my household gods to Heaven,
and I leave you, never to set eyes on you again."

I seemed to be looking on at a play. But since they were unconscious of being watched, for whose benefit was it these two marionettes
were acting this tragedy? The attitudes and gestures of the daughter
seemed to me as exaggerated and as artificial as those of the mother.
. . . The latter was facing me, so that I saw Isabelle from behind,
still prostrate in the posture of a suppliant Esther; all at once I caught
sight of her feet; the boots she wore, as far as I could see through
the coating of mud that covered them, seemed to have tops of puce
coloured poult-de-soie; above them showed her white stockings, across
which the dripping, muddy flounce of her lifted skirt had left a smear

of dirt. . . . And instantly the long story of adventure and wretchedness told by these poor witnesses spoke more loudly to my heart than all the old woman's declamatory tirades. A sob rose in my throat; I made up my mind to follow Isa through the garden when she left the house.

In the mean time Madame de Saint-Auréol had taken three steps towards Madame Floche's chair:

"Come, give me up those notes. Do you imagine I do not see the paper you are crumpling in your hand? Do you think me blind or mad? Give me the money, I tell you!" And seizing the notes, she held them melodramatically to the flame of one of the candles in the candelabra: "I would rather burn them all" (needless to say, she did nothing of the sort) "than let her have a groat."

She slipped the notes into her pocket and resumed her theatrical attitude:

"Ungrateful daughter! Unnatural daughter! My bracelets and my necklaces, you know what road they took! Let my rings go the same way!"

So saying, with a dexterous movement of her outstretched hand, she let two or three drop on to the floor. Like a famished dog after a bone, Isabelle flung herself upon them.

"Now go! We have nothing more to say to each other; I no longer acknowledge you."

Then, having fetched an extinguisher from the bedtable, she extinguished one after the other all the candles in the candelabra and departed.

The composition of these *récits* shows great narrative mastery in the chronological organization of events, in the rhythm of the scenes, in the progression of effects. In *L'Immoraliste*, Michel's cure is a wild *allegro* balanced by Marceline's death march, her persistent agony; between these two sections, rising and falling, occurs something of a plateau, formed by Michel's experiments in normal life; but this central portion is itself composed like the whole; Michel's attempts at being a landowner and his dawning disgust with the property frame the exalting conversations with Ménalque which determine the hero's orientation. In *La Porte étroite* it is enough to mention in passing the double illumination of facts by Jérôme's narrative and by Alissa's journal or her letters, with the deepening the latter produce in the former's pathos. Jérôme's narrative of the ruined walk is followed by the letter from Alissa it inspired. Similarly Jérôme's unhoped-for return during the night is presented from two complementary perspectives. And the asceticism by whose light Alissa believes she must send Jérôme away can be understood entirely only if we compare it with the young man's terror at the heroic dissimulation confessed in the young mystic's journal. Neither of the two knows everything about the other; it is only at the book's end that Jérôme will have, too late, a complete comprehension of a situation whose interest Gide has doubled by giving us Alissa's heart-rending journal.

The organization of *Isabelle* is even more skillful; it presents the facts not according to their genesis, but according to the order of their discovery, and this permits the narrator to maintain his illusions while disturbing him by unexplained details, and finally deflates them by the revelation of the banal reality. The composition of *La Symphonie pastorale* is more on one level, advancing steadily, although we can observe a series of parallels between events and their moral effects in Gertrude's transition from blindness to sight at the same time as from happiness to despair, and in the pastor, from blind exaltation to the bitter consciousness whose expression gives a contrasting tone to his two notebooks.—Notebooks kept by the pastor during the wintertime and spring in La Brévine;—Gérard's tale told to his friends Jammes and Gide after their conversation and visit to La Quartfourche;—recollections written by Jérôme, frequently alternating with fragments of Alissa's letters and, before the appendix of the journey to Nîmes, concluded by the pages of Alissa's journal;—Michel's narrative to his friends at night on the terrace of his house at Sidi B. M.—these are the means of presentation Gide uses with an equal ease. Despite the ingenuity of the breaks, the interruptions that he contrives in the notebooks and diaries to indicate a sudden change, a development, or the effect of time on the feelings, some readers may prefer to this mosaic the continuity of an ampler narrative. Nothing equals the splendid drive of *L'Immoraliste*. If the subtlety is greater in *La Porte étroite*, Gide himself, who was unable to return to it "without an unspeakable emotion," complains, with splendid frankness, that "the transitions" are not "exempt from preciosity." To make us discern the pastor's pious comedy on himself by giving us only his journal is a virtuoso performance; we may prefer that the progressive disclosure of the truth be effected with less cleverness, by the very progress of the narrative, as in *Isabelle*. Gide's art is eminently concerted, and it is of course when this organization is invisible that it functions most effectively.

Economy of means is another quality of this art of the *récit*. In Gide, every line counts. None is without its edge. From this point of view, *L'Immoraliste* is of a magnificent hardness and speed, whereas in *La Porte étroite* there are certain rare places that seem somewhat overworked, a little too satisfied with their own effects.

But where Gide excels is in the reverberation, the *reprise* of a detail; the reader will recall the scissors stolen by Moktir which are later found and returned to Michel by Ménalque. How one and the same sentence can affect the development of a soul according to the different values attributed to its meaning is shown in *L'Immoraliste* by a remark made by Marceline to Michel, and which he later addresses to Ménalque. The art of preparations, whose power is particularly prized in the theater, is no less necessary to the novel, but gains in discretion without losing any of its suggestiveness. Consider, for instance, how the second of these two passages is cruelly sensitized by the recollection of the first:

> Antoine, Etienne and Godefroi were discussing the last vote in the Chamber, as they lolled on my wife's elegant armchairs. Hubert and Louis were carelessly turning over some fine etchings from my father's collection, entirely regardless of how they were creasing them. In the smoking-room, Mathias, the better to listen to Léonard, had put his red-hot cigar down on a rosewood table. A glass of curaçoa had been spilt on the carpet. Albert was sprawling impudently on a sofa, with his muddy boots dirtying the cover. And the very dust of the air one breathed came from the horrible wear and tear of material objects. . . . A frantic desire seized me to send all my guests packing. Furniture, stuffs, prints, lost all their value for me at the first stain; things stained were things touched by disease, with the mark of death on them.

Here is the second passage:

> Meanwhile the horrible clot had brought on serious trouble; after her heart had escaped, it attacked her lungs, brought on congestion, impeded her breathing, made it short and laborious. I thought she would never get well. Disease had taken hold of Marceline, never again to leave her; it had marked her, stained her. Henceforth she was a thing that had been spoiled.

By making his main characters speak or write, Gide has obliged them to paint their own portraits. A method which admirably suits the tale and perfectly justifies (etymologically) the title *récit* that Gide affects. It was essential to lend each of these narrators a tone of his own. Here Gide's sympathy has served him further. His method seems indeed to have consisted of *listening* in himself to

the voice of his characters. Hence that timbre, those particular inflec-
tions which make us recognize them so certainly, without Gide's having to bother with all those clumsy "he saids" which encumber the
prose of novelists incapable of giving their protagonists a characteristic tone. Michel's harsh, unconceding tone, Gérard's *interested*
tone, Jérôme's fervent and rather suave tone, Alissa's ardent, secret,
strained and yet bare tone, the pastor's pious and somehow complacent tone—all are of an admirable rightness we must particularly
admire in the nuances and tacks of emotion.

The characters described by the narrators also have their own
tone, dissonances that are to be integrated into the basic tone. They
make it more apparent, as Abel's expansiveness contrasts with
Jérôme's reserve; or they complement it, as the characters' outbursts
in *Isabelle* set off Gérard's polished and amused moderation. Consider if, in Michel's tone, we succeed better than the man who tells
his story in distinguishing "pride's share from that of strength, of
coldness, or of modesty?":

> It had been very cold that morning. Toward evening a burning
> simoon sprang up. Marceline, exhausted by the journey, went to bed
> as soon as we arrived. I had hoped to find a rather more comfortable
> hotel, but our room is hideous; the sand, the sun, the flies have tar-
> nished, dirtied, discolored everything. As we have eaten scarcely any-
> thing since daybreak, I order a meal to be served at once; but Mar-
> celine finds everything uneatable and I cannot persuade her to touch
> a morsel. We have with us paraphernalia for making our own tea. I
> attend to this trifling business, and for dinner we content ourselves
> with a few biscuits and the tea, made with the brackish water of the
> country and tasting horrible in consequence.
>
> By a last semblance of virtue, I stay with her till evening. And all of
> a sudden I feel that I myself have come to the end of my strength. O
> taste of ashes! O deadly lassitude! O the sadness of superhuman effort!
> I hardly dare look at her; I am too certain that my eyes, instead of
> seeking hers, will fasten horribly on the black holes of her nostrils;
> the suffering expression of her face is agonizing. Nor does she look at
> me either. I feel her anguish as if I could touch it. She coughs a great
> deal and then falls asleep. From time to time, she is shaken by a sud-
> den shudder.
>
> Perhaps the night will be bad, and before it is too late I must find
> out where I can get help. I go out.
>
> Outside the hotel, the Touggourt square, the streets, the very at-
> mosphere, are so strange that I can hardly believe it is I who see
> them. After a little I go in again. Marceline is sleeping quietly. I
> need not have been so frightened; in this peculiar country, one sus-

pects peril everywhere. Absurd! And more or less reassured, I again go out.

There is a strange nocturnal animation in the square—a silent flitting to and fro—a stealthy gliding of white burnouses. The wind at times tears off a shred of strange music and brings it from I know not where. Someone comes up to me. . . . Moktir! He was waiting for me, he says—expected me to come out again. He laughs. He knows Touggourt, comes here often, knows where to take me. I let myself be guided by him.

We walk along in the dark and go into a Moorish café; this is where the music came from. Some Arab women are dancing—if such a monotonous glide can be called dancing. One of them takes me by the hand; I follow her; she is Moktir's mistress; he comes too. . . . We all three go into the deep, narrow room where the only piece of furniture is a bed. . . . A very low bed on which we sit down. A white rabbit which has been shut up in the room is scared at first but afterwards grows tamer and comes to feed out of Moktir's hand. Coffee is brought. Then, while Moktir is playing with the rabbit, the woman draws me toward her, and I let myself go to her as one lets oneself sink into sleep. . . .

Oh, here I might deceive you or be silent—but what use can this story be to me, if it ceases to be truthful?

I go back alone to the hotel, for Moktir remains behind in the café. It is late. A parching sirocco is blowing; the wind is laden with sand, and, in spite of the night, torrid. After three or four steps, I am bathed in sweat; but I suddenly feel I must hurry and I reach the hotel almost at a run. She is awake perhaps. . . . Perhaps she wants me? . . . No; the window of her room is dark. I wait for a short lull in the wind before opening the door; I go into the room very softly in the dark. What is that noise? . . . I do not recognize her cough. . . . Is it really Marceline? . . . I light the light.

She is half sitting on the bed, one of her thin arms clutching the bars and supporting her in an upright position; her sheets, her hands, her nightdress are flooded with a stream of blood; her face is soiled with it; her eyes have grown hideously big; and no cry of agony could be more appalling than her silence.

In *La Symphonie pastorale* we can admire how the pastor's tone, when he admonishes his elder son, can dissimulate his unconscious jealousy under the virtuous indignation he believes he is suffering. Finally I would point out as especially interesting the effects of tone *against* tone. The sublime fervor of Alissa surpasses, but often accompanies, Jérôme's more tepid but nonetheless sincere fervor. Ménalque's conversation with Michel marks, in the two characters, two degrees of a related but still unequal tension.

We need not insist on the point. Gide's style here retains all the qualities we have discerned in his poetic prose. But since it is the expression of characters who say "I" but are not Gide, the language is barer, soberer, more direct, and carefully avoids those *recherché* turns of speech and those violations of syntax by which Gide inflects his own sentences. These are not artists talking; these are human beings. But here too Gide never forgets that art is transposition; and the perfect stylization of his characters' dialogue shows that while respecting the particularity of their personal idiom, the author purifies it in order to render it still more faithful to his meaning, and raises it, by the finish he imparts to it, to the level of art, whose truth is less that of reproduction than that of representation.

Passionate yet measured; their composition so clear and sober, their passion so contained, their *attention* so loving, their diligence so skillful; stripped of all superfluity (one only appreciates to what degree Gide's tales are without digression when one reads other storytellers), these *récits* irresistibly remind us of the great portrait painters of the French school, especially, perhaps, in their exclusion of pomp and prettiness and sentimentality, of the perfect honesty of a Clouet.

A New Reading of Gide's *La Porte étroite*

by Loring D. Knecht

It is all too tempting on first acquaintance with Gide's *La Porte étroite* to see in it only the pathetically tragic tale of a young girl who believed too wholeheartedly that "virtue is its own reward." Not too surprising, for this seems to be the reaction Gide intended to elicit. He protested against the view of some critics that he had "evolved" to a more sympathetic moral and religious attitude since 1902 and the publication of *L'Immoraliste*.[1] He insisted repeatedly that he sought rather to make the work a criticism of a certain furiously deplorable protestantism, a puritanism that curiously evokes Jansenism, a misplaced sense of heroism which he characterizes as a sort of "gratuitous Cornelianism." [2] This last must certainly apply to Alissa rather than to Jérôme.

That Gide thought it necessary to provide some plausible exterior motivation for Alissa's taking the path of ascetic puritanism is clear in a letter written to Paul Claudel in June 1909:

> This drama would not emerge in all its purity unless the element of external constraint were entirely removed. But I was afraid that, if all external motivation were discarded, it would seem paradoxical,

"A New Reading of Gide's *La Porte étroite*," by Loring D. Knecht. From PMLA, LXXXII, no. 7 (December, 1967), 640–48. Copyright © 1967 by the Modern Language Association of America. Reprinted by permission of the author and the Modern Language Association of America. Passages from Gide's works cited in French in the original essay are here translated into English.

[1] André Gide, *Journal, 1889–1939*, Pléiade edition (Paris: Gallimard, 1948), pp. 365–66, 428–29, 437—hereafter cited as *Journal I*.

[2] *Paul Claudel et André Gide, Correspondance, 1899–1926* (Paris: Gallimard, 1949), p. 90 (17 Oct. 1908); pp. 103–4 (18 June 1909). See also *Journal I*, pp. 428–29 (30 June 1914): "Whether tales or satirical farces, I have written up to now nothing but ironic—or, if you wish, critical—works, of which this [i.e., *Les Caves du Vatican*] is probably the last. There is a certain amusement and even some advantage in letting the critics make a mistake at first. But how could I be surprised that they didn't see at once that my *Porte étroite* was a critical work?"

if not monstrous and inhuman. So I invented the double intrigue, the fear of buying her happiness at the cost of the happiness of somebody else—and, above all, the mother's "crime," and the resulting vague need of expiation and so forth.[3]

It is understandable that statements of this type should have thrown critics somewhat off the track. Yet, it does appear strange that, although most have seemed keenly aware of the "elusive Proteus" that is Gide, few if any have been finely enough attuned to the subtly elusive ambiguity of this particular *récit*. Alissa has been reduced to too much of a "deliberate simplification," a girl who destroys the possibility of realizing her normal potential as a woman by a precocious and rather unnatural renunciation of earthly happiness in favor of a heavenly ideal. A drama of mistaken virtue, giving the Gide of *L'Immoraliste* the chance to balance the earthy excesses revealed in that work with a work criticizing the excesses of ascetic, unearthly puritanism. Gide suggests this in an entry in his *Journal* dated 7 February 1912, three years after the publication of *La Porte étroite*: "Whom could I persuade that the book is the twin of *L'Immoraliste* and that the two subjects grew up concurrently in my mind, the excess of one finding a secret permission in the excess of the other and together establishing a balance" (*Journal I*, pp. 365–66).

This *récit* would then be the simply and artlessly told account of the distillation of a religious essence which, burning too brightly, devours its own flame with ever-increasing intensity as Alissa withdraws bafflingly and by almost imperceptible degrees, but in "a single direction"[4] from the real world of Jérôme, the man she loves. The final irony: without her love, Jérôme, she can not finally find peace in her saintly sacrifice (for she had thought to remove herself as a barrier between Jérôme and God) and dies alone, bereft of even the God she had adored. A classical debate between love and duty, duty to her religion, to her God, one might suppose. No. As is the case with the Princess of Clèves in Madame de La Fayette's seventeenth-century novel, the real motivation lies elsewhere than in an apparent sense of duty.

If we are to assess the true center of gravity of *La Porte ètroite*, its true density, we must be fully alert to the startling contrast pre-

[3] *Paul Claudel et André Gide, Correspondance*, p. 104 (18 June 1909).
[4] Germaine Brée, *Gide* (New Brunswick, N. J.: Rutgers Univ. Press, 1963), p. 153—hereafter cited as Brée.

sented in the very beginning of the novel between the character of Jérôme and that of Alissa. We must be conscious of the harmonics of every word as we hear now the informed hints of the Narrator (an older Jérôme recounting the story ten years after the death of Alissa), now the reactions and uncomprehending reflections of the younger Jérôme quoted directly from the midst of the action. The earliest portraits of Jérôme and Alissa are crucial in this respect. Here Gide has given us the point of departure with disarming frankness and honesty. There is a most charming air of freshness and naturalness in our first impression of Alissa as furnished by the Narrator:

> That Alissa Bucolin was pretty, I was incapable yet of perceiving; I was drawn and held to her by a charm other than mere beauty. . . . I like to fancy that Beatrice as a child had eyebrows wide-arched like hers. They gave her look, her whole being, an expression of enquiry which was at once anxious and confident—yes, of passionate enquiry. She was all question and expectation.[5]

The implication is that of a warm, extremely feminine personality who lives in the expectation that life holds in store delicious moments waiting to be tasted. Far from seeing in Alissa a virtue that is "forced" or "excessive" (to fit with the impression that Gide always maintained he had wanted to give),[6] she is revealed to us a bit further on as having a virtue that "seemed like relaxation, so much there was in it of ease and grace." "Everything in her unaffected and artless soul," he says in completing her portrait, "was of the most natural beauty" (p. 507). How startlingly similar to the evocation of his wife Madeleine made late in life in his revelations in *Et nunc manet in te:* "Everything in her wished only to blossom forth sweetly and tenderly. . . . It is for that reason that I cannot console myself" (*Et nunc,* p. 1148). Gide's protestations to the contrary notwithstanding (*Et nunc,* p. 1148), Alissa *is* to a remarkable degree Madeleine.[7]

And what of our introduction to Jérôme? His first real portrait is preceded by the significant incident between Jérôme and Alissa's mother, the Creole Lucile Bucolin. This passionate, this gay and

[5] André Gide, *La Porte étroite,* in *Romans, récits et soties,* Pléiade edition (Paris: Gallimard, 1958), p. 501—subsequent references will be made in text.

[6] André Gide, *Et nunc manet in te* in *Journal (1939–1949), Souvenirs,* Pléiade edition (Paris: Gallimard, 1954), p. 1148—hereafter cited as *Et nunc.*

[7] Perhaps one might rather say that Madeleine is Alissa. The resignation that Jérôme imposed on Alissa was later to be imposed on Gide's wife Madeleine.

loose woman inspires a physical terror of women in the young
Jérôme (about fourteen or fifteen years old) when she lasciviously
caresses him one hot summer day:

> . . . She drew my face down to hers, passed her bare arm around
> my neck, put her hand into my shirt, asked me laughingly if I was
> ticklish—went on—further. . . . I started so violently that my shirt
> tore across and with a flaming face I fled, as she called after me.
> "Oh! the little stupid!"
> I rushed away to the other end of the kitchen-garden, and there I
> dipped my handkerchief into a little tank, put it to my forehead—
> washed, scrubbed—my cheeks, my neck, every part of me the woman
> had touched (p. 500).

Small wonder the Narrator, looking back over the years, should
exclaim bitterly: "Lucile Bucolin, I wish I no longer bore you
malice; I wish I could forget for a moment how much harm you
did . . ." (p. 499). It only remains to the alert reader to imagine
what this harm must be and to follow its effects throughout the
novel. Gide is too conscious an artist to let such a loaded word fall by
accident. Jérôme has been soiled by premature physical contact with
Woman in the person of his wayward Aunt Lucile. This harm, its
effect on Jérôme, will be important in determining the future course
of his relationship with his cousin Alissa.

Not long after this incident, as Jérôme is climbing the stairs to
Alissa's room, he passes his Aunt Lucile's open door and is shocked
to see her playing host to a young lieutenant in what is obviously a
love tryst. In a flash, the laughter and gayety coming from the room
are indelibly associated in his mind with sin, with physical love
between man and woman as represented in the illicit relationship
between Lucile Bucolin and her lover. He rushes to Alissa's room,
finds her in tears, and dedicates his life to her: "Drunken with love,
with pity, with an indistinguishable mixture of enthusiasm, of self-
sacrifice, of virtue, I appealed to God with all my strength—I offered
myself up to Him, unable to conceive that existence could have any
other object than to shelter this child from fear, from evil, from
life" (p. 504). Two days later, Jérôme is to see his cousin Alissa and
her sister Juliette in church and attaches great importance to this
"sanctification" of their meeting. The sermon text, taken from the
words of Christ, "Strive to enter in at the strait gate" (Luke 13:24)
inspires in him a daydream in which he fancies the strait gate, that
is the *narrow* gate, as "a sort of press" into which he passes "with
an extremity of pain" (p. 505). This gate becomes for him the door

of Alissa's room. At the end of the sermon, rather than approaching Alissa, he flees her, thinking so best to deserve her.

The more mature Jérôme, the Narrator, looking back on this incident, gives the first portrait of his younger self while explaining why he should have been thus affected:

> This austere teaching found my soul ready prepared and naturally predisposed to duty. My father's and mother's example, added to the puritanical discipline to which they had submitted the earliest impulses of my heart, inclined me still more towards what I used to hear called "virtue." Self-control was as natural to me as self-indulgence to others, and this severity to which I was subjected, far from being irksome to me, was soothing. It was not so much happiness which I sought in the future, as the infinite effort to attain it, and in my mind I already confounded happiness with virtue (p. 506).

Not only has Jérôme thought to deserve Alissa better by avoiding her, he now offers up to her mystically work, efforts, pious acts, and invents a "refinement of virtue" by which he often leaves her in ignorance of what he has done only for her sake. Indeed, he feels no satisfaction in anything that does not cost him an effort (p. 507).

Should we, by some strange inattention, not have noticed that it is Jérôme who first points out the path to ascetic religious sublimation, how could we fail to note the central importance of the ensuing comments connected with the portrait of Alissa with which we are already familiar: "Was I alone to feel the spur of emulation? I do not think that Alissa was touched by it, or that she did anything for my sake or for me, though all my efforts were only for her. Everything in her unaffected and artless soul was of the most natural beauty. Her virtue seemed like relaxation, so much there was in it of ease and grace" (p. 507). It would be impossible to imagine a greater contrast with the portrait the Narrator has made of his younger self. Not only does he specifically point out to us that Alissa did not, in the beginning, share in his ascetic sublimation, but it is no accident that every word of this most captivating portrait of his cousin forms a kind of counterpoint to the portrait he has previously made of himself. "Her unaffected and artless soul," "the most natural beauty," summed up in a virtue that "seemed like relaxation." How like Shakespeare's mercy, the quality of which is not strained. And how far we are from foreseeing the possibility that Alissa may take the lead along the hard and rocky path of associating self-denial, abnegation with ultimate virtue. It is Jérôme who, by avoiding her, by leaving her in ignorance of what he does for her sake, suggests to her that their relationship is not apt to lead to a full and normal union.

Soon after, Jérôme's mother dies. Curiously enough, although he loved his mother deeply, Jérôme wondered that he should feel so little sadness, noting that if he wept, it was out of pity for his mother's companion, Miss Ashburton, who felt the loss so keenly (p. 512). Does the reader detect a curious lack in Jérôme, who seems to be able to experience only by ricochet an emotion that most would feel directly?

It has quite often been asserted, to show Alissa as leading the way in her relationship with Jérôme, that she is responsible for continually deferring their engagement. It is rather Jérôme. When quizzed by Alissa's younger sister Juliette, he not only fails to sense that she too is in love with him (what manner of man is he?), but replies in this fashion to her questions as to when he and Alissa will marry: "Not before I've done my military service. And indeed, not before I have a better idea of what I mean to do afterwards."

"Don't you know yet?"

"I don't want to know yet. Too many things appeal to me. I want to put off for as long as I can having to choose and settle down to only one thing" (p. 517–18). Juliette probes further: "Is it reluctance to settle down that makes you put off getting engaged too?" The Narrator continues: "I shrugged my shoulders without answering." It is hardly surprising that, when Jérôme says, "I should only want to be engaged if I distrusted her," Juliette should reply with brutal frankness, "It isn't Alissa that I distrust . . ." (p. 518).

What more do we need to establish Jérôme's insufficiency, or at any rate, his unreliability as a lover and suitor? He not only seems completely unresponsive to, indeed unaware of Juliette's very warm physical presence and gives evidence of wishing to place his love for Alissa on the level of an unattainable ideal, but he is even evasive on the purely practical level, showing an unwillingness to choose and fix his attention on one object. And Alissa has overheard the whole of the conversation between Jérôme and Juliette, sensing not only the elusive quality of Jérôme's love for her (as had Juliette), but further the fact that Juliette is deeply in love with him. The latter might not have taken on so much importance for Alissa had she not been made aware of the former. Jérôme-Narrator is careful to help us note this: "Ah! blind wretch that I was, groping after my own errors, not to have thought for a moment that Juliette's words, to which I had paid so little attention, and which I remembered so

ill, might perhaps have been better understood by Alissa" (p. 520).
The next day Jérôme is to return to Paris. When, in the morning,
he knocks at Alissa's door, he is utterly unconvincing in what he
thinks is an offer of engagement: "The word 'engagement' seemed
to me too bare, too brutal; I used I know not what periphrase in
its stead" (p. 521). He is not exactly an aggressive suitor, one a girl
would feel secure in leaning on. It should come as no surprise to
the reader that Alissa asks him in reply: "Why change?" And well
she might ask, not because she would like to delay their engagement,
but has she not overheard him tell Juliette that he saw no reason
to change their relationship, that it was not time to settle down?
In a most touching scene, revealing the intensity of Alissa's emotion
throughout, she finally tears him gently from her—and he lets her
do it (p. 521).

It remains for Jérôme's friend Abel Vautier to confirm for us the
import of this scene. Far from thinking that Alissa might have
decided that she will never marry Jérôme, that she will stay single
because of a preoccupation with religious asceticism, he sees it all
simply as a case of a lack of aggressiveness in the would-be lover:
"He [Abel Vautier] laughed at me for not having finally managed
to clinch the matter, as he expressed it, giving forth as an axiom,
that a woman should never be given time to go back on herself"
(p. 522). Although Jérôme did not consider this argument applicable
to him and his cousin, the reader, maintaining (as he must) a certain detachment from the Narrator, may well disagree. When Abel
exclaims, "To tell you the truth, there's something I can't understand in your tale; you can't have told me everything. . . ." (p.
523), he calls to mind inevitably Jérôme's "flabby character," which
Gide himself was the first to admit (*Journal I*, p. 276, 7 November
1909). But, had Jérôme been able to take Abel's advice, Gide's novel
would not have been possible.

By now, Alissa has begun, perhaps unconsciously, to express her
disappointment in Jérôme by means of a modest withdrawal in
which she takes refuge in the phrases Jérôme has taught her, repeating in a letter to their Aunt Plantier that "arduous duty" uplifts
the soul (p. 542). But the tone of her whole letter is that of a warm,
passionate being reaching out for the only love that can make her
complete. Every line is in reality meant for Jérôme as Abel Vautier
points out to his friend. Has Alissa already gone too far upon the
path of idealistic ascetic puritanism to turn back? In a sudden insight, she declares that she now really understands the meaning of

the Bible verse: "Cursed be the man that trusteth in men" (p. 543). Why the sudden insight? Jérôme himself had signaled it to her: she found the verse on a Christmas card he had given her years before. She senses that her earthly happiness can not be that of a normal and complete union with Jérôme; she can not trust in man, that is, in Jérôme. He had had the habit of putting the initial of her name alongside passages that he wished her to note, most of them passages leading her down the path of religious abnegation rather than human fulfillment (p. 545). And yet, in the eyes of the red-blooded young observer, Abel Vautier, it is still not too late to avert tragedy. When Jérôme confides to him that Alissa does not seem to be taking the right road, Abel applies the natural corrective: "It only depends upon you for her to take it!" (p. 544).

It is certainly hard to think that Abel is wrong when Alissa, in her letters sent to Jérôme while he is traveling, utters heartrending soul-cries that tell us from which quarter she would like her happiness to come:

> Whenever I think of you, my heart fills with hope. [. . .] Sometimes I look for you involuntarily [. . .] And suddenly I wanted you there —I felt you there, close to me—with such violence that perhaps you felt it. [. . .] I think of the radiant land Juliette speaks of. I think of other lands, vaster, more radiant still, more desert-like. A *strange* conviction dwells in me that one day—but I cannot tell how—you and I shall see together some great mysterious land . . . (p. 547).

It is perhaps not really too late, but Alissa is at the crossroads. The symbolism seems clear: will she weigh anchor and travel with Jérôme to the mysterious land of love, or will the only radiant land for her be Heaven? At this point she can not tell which. She is waiting for Jérôme to convince her.

The reaction of Jérôme to this appeal would be incomprehensible but for the fact that we have already come to appreciate his "flabby" nature:

> Alissa, it is true, thanked me for not coming to Fongueusemare; it is true she begged me not to try to see her again that year, but she regretted my absence, she wanted me; from page to page there sounded the same appeal. Where did I find strength to resist it? In Abel's advice, no doubt, and in the fear of suddenly ruining my joy, and in an instinctive stiffening of my will against the inclinations of my heart (pp. 547–48).

This time Jérôme's problem is not blindness as it so often is. He is lucid as, playing his role of the Narrator, he looks back and asks: "Where did I find strength to resist it?" "Where indeed?" we are inevitably prompted to exclaim. And from what depths comes this fear of ruining his joy, this instinctive stiffening of his will? We should not be too surprised when we recall the young Jérôme's terrifying experience with his aunt, Lucile Bucolin, when we recall also the earliest portrait we have of him and his natural disposition toward discipline and self-constraint.

Alissa's letters keep coming in a steady stream, the accents of each one more poignant, more passionate than the last. She imagines herself with him on his travels in Italy and exclaims: "Oh, my friend! It is through you that I look at all things. How much I like what you write about St. Francis! Yes, what we should seek for is indeed—*is it not?* [italics mine]—an exaltation and not an emancipation of the mind. The latter goes only with an abominable pride. Our ambition should lie not in revolt but in service" (p. 548). Before giving expression to her passionate longings, she is testing Jérôme to see whether he still wants her to proceed in the direction of ascetic Christian sublimation. She looks at all things only through Jérôme, but what is the sense of the intercalated question "is it not?" if not a probe to test whether Jérôme might not now be willing to turn in another direction?

Once having said what she thinks Jérôme wants to hear (he has in reality suggested it to her), she gives expression to the most ingenuous and genuine urges of her being: "This evening I am writing as in a dream—and all I realize is an almost oppressive sense of infinite riches to bestow and to receive" (p. 548–49). And, feeling that a closer contact has been established with him, she continues: "Now that I have found you again, life, thought, our souls—everything seems beautiful, adorable, inexhaustibly fertile. . . ." It would be hard to imagine accents more revealing of the natural woman that is Alissa! Her religious asceticism is thoroughly mixed with elemental, earthy joy. "The day before yesterday I took an enormously long walk, going across country at random. When I came in I was not so much tired as excited, almost intoxicated with sun and joy." She hears and understands "Nature's 'mingled hymn,' " but all her sensuous outbursts are confused with religious mysticism: "Yes, dear friend, it is as you say, an exhortation to joy which I hear and understand in Nature's 'mingled hymn.' I hear it in every bird's song; I breathe it in the scent of every flower, and I have reached the point of conceiving adoration as the only form of prayer, repeating over and over again with St. Francis: 'My God! My God! *e non altro'*—and nothing else—my heart filled with *inexpressible* love" (p. 549). But this "inexpressible love," is it really directed only to God? Has Alissa not already revealed its true object in writing at the same time of "infinite riches to bestow and receive," of life becoming once again for her "inexhaustibly fertile"? This is not the vocabulary of heavenly love, but of human love.

But when Christmas draws near, and with it the possibility of seeing one another, there is a strange hiatus in their communication. It is hard to be satisfied with the explanation of Jérôme-Narrator as he tells why they decided not to meet (at least he attributes the decision to both of them). It was, he says, "out of a sort of spirit of defiance, which made us deliberately prolong our time of waiting— out of fear, too, of an unsatisfactory meeting" (p. 551). The Alissa of the letters to Italy could not really have wished for this postponement.

As time wears on into the following year, the joyful tone of Alissa's earlier letters changes to one of anguish, of desperation, as though nothing can mean anything to her without Jérôme: "Oh, my brother! I am only truly myself—more than myself—when I am with you. . . . Every day that has to be got through before I see you again weighs on me, oppresses me. [. . .]My books are without virtue and without charm; my walks have no attraction; Nature has lost her glamour; the garden is emptied of color, of scent" (pp. 552, 554). Even her health seems to be affected: "I have not been quite so well lately; oh! nothing serious. I think I am just looking forward to your coming a little too much" (p. 554). These are not the accents of religious sublimation; but Alissa is for some reason afraid, in advance, that their coming meeting will be no more fruitful than those in the past. Sensing no haste on Jérôme's part, she gives him a way out, saying that he need not feel he has to stay more than a couple of days and concludes with, "Shall we not have all our lives?" (p. 555). Such a question from an insecure woman requires a positive answer: "No!" But it will not be forthcoming. Their meeting is physically awkward; they are unable to talk to one another; Jérôme does not speak of an engagement. "Alissa," says the Narrator, "unable to bear it, and with her eyes full of tears, alleged a violent headache, and we drove home in silence" (p. 557). This is the final deception for her. After Jérôme has returned to Paris, she writes him:

"My friend, what a melancholy meeting! You seemed to lay the blame on other people, but without being able to convince yourself. And now I think—I know—it will be so always. Oh! I beg of you, don't let us see each other again!

"Why this awkwardness, this feeling of being in a false position, this paralysis, this dumbness, when we have everything in the world to say to each other? The first day of your return this very silence made me happy, because I believed it would vanish, and that you would tell me the most wonderful things; it was impossible that you should leave me without doing so" (p. 558).

But he did leave her without speaking of an engagement, without speaking of that mysterious land of love for which she is longing to weigh anchor. It was his place as the man to speak, to break the silence, to tell her wonderful things. After that, how can Alissa feel any hope, how can she believe in his love, in his virility, or in her own charms? She now must believe that he does not really love her, or at any rate, that he does not love her as she feels she must be loved if they are ever to marry with any chance of real happiness. And she adds a postscript: "I do not wish to let this letter go without asking you to show a little more discretion in regard to what concerns us both. Many a time you have wounded me by talking to Juliette or Abel about things which should have remained private between you and me, and this is, indeed, what made me think—long before you suspected it—that your love was above all intellectual, the beautiful tenacity of a tender faithful mind" (p. 559). Jérôme's answer, protesting that he loves her with his whole soul and heart, still does nothing to convince her that he might love her physically. And then, somehow, we get the impression that it is all too easy for him to put it out of his mind: "as soon as my letter had gone I was able to bury myself in my work" (p. 560). When Jérôme next meets Alissa, it is Easter time and he finds her in the garden. She stretches out her arms to him and puts her hands on his shoulders—and what is Jérôme's first utterance? "Listen, Alissa, I have twelve days before me. I will not stay one more than you please. Let us settle on a sign, which shall mean: 'Tomorrow you must leave Fongueusemare'" (p. 562). That can hardly be what Alissa was waiting to hear. She tests him by asking, "But will you be able to go without a tear or a sigh?" (p. 562). Incredibly, he replies, "Without a good-bye. I shall leave you on that last evening exactly as I shall have done the evening before, so simply that you will wonder whether I have understood." And he adds, "But from now till that fatal evening, not an allusion to make me feel that it is coming" (p. 562). The responsibility for the fatality that hovers over their relationship has to be Jérôme's. By his brutal choice of language he has (one wonders how consciously) warned Alissa that the "fatal evening" *will* come, that it is entirely within his power to leave her, and what is even more astounding, to leave her without a tear, a sigh, or a good-bye. And not only does he say he can do this, he actually does it (p. 564).

It is only after this incredible proof of bloodlessness and insensitivity that Alissa writes to Jérôme with the unmistakable indication that she must seek her happiness elsewhere. "Good-bye, my friend, *Hic incipit amor Dei*. Ah! will you ever know how much I love you? . . . Until the end I will be your ALISSA" (p. 565). And the Narrator himself, the Jérôme of ten years later, is at this point either still insensitive or lacking in frankness, for he dares maintain: "Against the snare of virtue I was defenseless" (p. 565). Their very correspondence must come to an end under such circumstances, but not before Alissa has underlined the final ambiguity of her position by writing: "But, my friend, holiness is not a choice; it is an obligation" (p. 565). And she had underlined three times the word *"obligation."* The reader now has two alternatives as to how to interpret this word *"obligation":* Does Alissa mean that her duty to God requires her to follow the path of holiness (seen as the suppression of all human interests in favor of complete concentration on the Creator)? Or doesn't she rather mean to convey to Jérôme that this path to sanctity has been forced upon her by her human situation, by the fact that Jérôme has not really offered her any other alternative? We would not expect the young Jérôme to catch such a double meaning—and he doesn't.

But what about the occasionally more perceptive Jérôme-Narrator? Not only does he see it as he looks back on the tragedy, but he accuses the callow self he once was:

> How should I, by a simple recital, make clear at once what I myself understood at first so ill? What can I paint here save the occasion of the wretchedness which from that moment overwhelmed me wholly? For if I have no forgiveness in my heart today for my failure to recognize that love that was still throbbing, hidden under a semblance so artificial, it was at first only this semblance that I was able to see; and so no longer finding my friend, I accused her . . . (p. 566).

In the face of such an admission, how is it possible to see the movement of Alissa toward ascetic puritanism to be of her own volition, rather than what it really was, an "artificial semblance"?

Not that Alissa was hypocritical. She was rather making a genuine effort to sublimate her unrequited love for Jérôme in a love for God—and (like Gide's wife Madeleine) with the delicate modesty natural to her did not want to make a maudlin display of this pathetic necessity: thus the dissimulation.

Alissa now consciously seeks to make Jérôme believe that she has suppressed all her artistic and intellectual interests. Surely this must be interpreted in the light of Jérôme's lack of aggressiveness, his lack of understanding. Despairing of ever arousing in him the physical love for her that she desires, she loses faith in her own attractiveness, in her own charms. She feels that he does not really love her. What does it matter to her then if she looks dowdy, if she appears to Jérôme to be uninterested in the art and poetry that are his constant preoccupation? All her earlier interests were tied up with her love for him. All she did, she did for him.[8] The "frightful obliteration of all poetry," as Jérôme calls it (p. 573), that appears to take place in her has a deeply human motivation and is certainly not just the evidence of ascetic mortification. And is it not, in a sense, a test of Jérôme? When he cries out, "Alissa! Alissa! it was you I loved. What have you done with yourself? What have you made yourself become?" doesn't she finally answer, "Jérôme, why don't you simply admit that you love me less?" (p. 572). Although Jérôme protests that this is not the case, this is what Alissa must believe. If he is now disappointed with her, it must have been that he was more in love with the outward interests they had in common than he was with her herself. She is but reconfirmed in her sad conviction that his is only a love of the head, "the beautiful tenacity of a tender faithful mind" (p. 559). She also has no concrete manifestations from him that would persuade her to the contrary. Indeed, the Narrator, when he left to teach in the School of Athens, found himself "welcoming the idea of departure as though it had been an escape" (p. 574).

The only evidence of any normal male aggressiveness in Jérôme comes when it is much too late. Three years later, he returns to find an Alissa literally wasted away, desiccated by the loss of her love, by the lack of any warm physical presence. The effort to consummate her enforced renunciation of a normal human relationship with the

---

[8] See *Et nunc,* p. 1137: Long after the publication of *La Porte étroite,* the same road is taken by Gide's wife Madeleine: "The truth is that she believed I had ceased to love her. From that time on, what was the use of embellishing herself to please me? As for pleasing me, there was no longer any point in thinking of it."

man she loves has cost her dearly. She is thin and pale and clings
to Jérôme "as though she were frightened or cold" (p. 576). It is
only now, when she has already wasted away almost beyond the point
of return, that he takes her in his arms and kisses her. (It is hard
to believe in this physical manifestation of love in Jérôme when
it is the only occurrence of this type in the whole novel.) Although
she is physically unresisting, she points out to Jérôme why it is too
late: "No, my friend, there is not time. There was no longer time
from the moment when our love made us foresee for one another
something better than love. *Thanks to you* [italics mine], my friend,
my dream climbed so high that any earthly satisfaction would have
been a descent. I have often thought of what our life with each other
would have been; as soon as it had been less than perfect, I could
not have borne . . . our love" (p. 578). The "Thanks to you" certainly enlightens us as to the responsibility Jérôme must bear in
the tragedy. And can Alissa possibly mean that she has found something better than their love? This would be hard to believe, for
after the two have walked in silence for a few moments we hear
her suddenly burst out: "Can you imagine it, Jérôme? 'Some better
thing!'" And suddenly tears start from her eyes as she repeats:
"'Some better thing!'" Why the tears if she does not see this as an
ironic, a tragic phrase? Obviously, she can not really believe that
there might be "some better thing." She is simply clinging des-
perately to what she believes to be her only hope of filling the void
that has been left in her life by the failure of Jérôme to love her in
the right way. As for her own feelings for Jérôme, the Narrator
reveals that when they parted her eyes were "filled with an unspeakable love" (p. 578).

Then follows one of the most curious and revealing passages in
the whole *récit* as told by the older Jérôme:

> As soon as the door was shut, as soon as I heard the bolt drawn
> behind her, I fell against the door, a prey to the extremest despair,
> and stayed for a long time weeping and sobbing in the night.
> But to have kept her, to have forced the door, to have entered by
> any means whatever into the house, which yet would not have been
> shut against me—no, even today, when I look back to the past and
> live it over again—no, it was not possible to me, and whoever does not
> understand me here, has understood nothing of me up till now (pp.
> 578–79).

And yet, when Jérôme the Narrator finally takes the reader more
completely into his confidence at the end of the novel and gives him

Alissa's diary to read, we discover that Alissa was waiting on the other side of that door, hoping passionately that he would force his way in. When Jérôme tells us that this was not possible for him, he explains nothing. Rather, to maintain the artistic integrity of his work, Gide dares to demand all from the perspicacity of the reader. If he has not been alert, if he does not want to understand, he will not understand, for the understanding can only come from a careful noting of the importance of Jérôme's true nature. That nature can be easily obscured by the more obvious emphasis on Alissa's progressive ascetic puritanism. The Narrator underscores that it is *he* whom we must understand if we are to see clearly, that we must be alert to the fact that something has forced him to recount the tale with a certain reticence. It is for us to guess that something. If we are hypnotized into following Alissa's development too exclusively, we will fail to understand.

Why was Jérôme never able to overcome Alissa's reticences, why was he never warm and physically responsive to her, why did he direct all her enquiring passion and expectation, her natural joy in life, in the direction of artistic and mystical idealization? Simply because he was not *able* to do otherwise. Not only are all the indications present as internal evidence, but Gide's striking revelations forty-three years later in *Et nunc manet in te* show us what an accurate foreshadowing of the problems of his own married life is to be found in *La Porte étroite*. Admitting that one of the main flaws in his love for his wife, Madeleine, had been its "thoughtlessness" and "blindness," he pursues: "I am amazed today at that aberration which led me to think that the more ethereal my love was, the more worthy it was of her—for I was so naïve as never to wonder whether or not she would be satisfied with an utterly disincarnate love" (*Et nunc*, p. 1128). We are now listening to what might well be a Jérôme-Narrator who has finally become absolutely frank:

> I wanted her happiness, to be sure, but did not think of this: that the happiness to which I wanted *to lead and force* her [italics mine] would be unbearable to her. Since she seemed to me all soul and, as far as the body was concerned, all fragility, I did not consider that it amounted to depriving her greatly to keep from her a part of me that I counted all the less important because I could not give it to her. . . . Between us no explanation was ever attempted. Never a complaint from her; nothing but mute resignation and an unconfessed rebuff (*Et nunc*, p. 1129).

Like Alissa, Gide's wife was too noble, and loved him too much, to be brutally frank with the man she loved. Neither woman indulges in wild outbursts of recrimination; there is, in the case of Alissa, only a valiant but tragic attempt at resignation and religious sublimation —tragic because there will be no final reconciliation, nor even any fulfillment on a spiritual plane. Alissa dies alone in a bare, rented room, but not before she has confided to her diary the most pathetic expression of her desire to recover her original virtue, made of grace and relaxation, a virtue that would not be at variance with love:

> How happy must that soul be for whom virtue is one with love! Sometimes I doubt whether there is any other virtue than love . . . to love as much as possible and continually more and more. . . . But at other times, alas! virtue appears to me to be nothing but resistance to love. What! Shall I dare to call "virtue" that which is the most natural inclination of my heart? Oh, tempting sophism! Specious allurement! Cunning mirage of happiness! (p. 586).

Yes, her dream of happiness was destined to be only a "cunning mirage," based as it was on the "ethereal" Jérôme. In the face of this fact, Gide's invention of what he called the "double intrigue" to give an "exterior motivation" to the drama (i.e., the ostensible reasons given by Alissa for her withdrawal into religious asceticism) seems almost unnecessary. A much more convincing motivation has been provided in her disappointment with Jérôme. In Gide's inability to keep from including, as a muted but persistent strain, the reflection of his own problem with his wife, he created a more complex rhythm and plot line than would otherwise have been the case. And it is precisely in the sinuous, elusive aspect which these communicate that the novel's lingering ambiguity is best expressed. The *sotto voce* comments of the Narrator, in effect warning us not to take all the protestations of Jérôme at face value, the triple optic of Jérôme's *récit* (i.e., the viewpoint of the young Jérôme; the reported selective coments from Alissa; the direct comments of the older Jérôme-Narrator) keep us in a proper state of indecision—so much so that even the perceptive reader must await the revelations of Alissa's diary at the end for full confirmation of his suspicions. The true function of Alissa's ostensible reasons now becomes apparent. In a sense, they are like the false clues of a detective novel, keeping up our interest and sweeping us along so that we will not too prematurely settle on the murderer. The Narrator admits that he has not given us all of Alissa's letters to read. Thus he reveals to us that he is not completely reliable, that he has held something back, and, in reality, invites us not to have complete confidence in him. When he has finished his tale, we discover why he has so invited us as he proffers us Alissa's diary. The doubts we may have had up to then must surely be dissipated by its desperate accents. The most passionate laments are those expressing her tragic disappointment at not having been able to reconcile virtue with love. The import of all her tentative, suggestive questions directed toward Jérôme (as reported by the Narrator in the *récit*) is now made clear in the light of the most intimate entries confided to her journal. They were desperate signals to Jérôme to break through and save her from the increasingly empty comfort of puritan asceticism. But Jérôme could not understand, he was not able to hear.

What is the function of Alissa's diary, coming to the reader as a complete surprise? Germaine Brée has called it an artificial surprise and has raised the question as to why the revelations of the diary were disregarded by the Narrator when he presumably has had the diary in his possession for some time (Brée, p. 154). If his story is indeed a simple and straightforward account, as he tells us on the opening page, then he should inform the whole with pertinent allusions to her diary. But what of Gide's basic artistic purpose? He no doubt hoped to recreate for the reader the feeling for the situation that existed at the time when the younger Jérôme was actively involved in the dramatic events. An important consideration would then be to give the impression of ambiguity that Jérôme himself must have felt, to oblige the reader to participate in Jérôme's self-delusion. This would not be possible if the reader were to have too early confirmation from Alissa's diary of those hints from the Narrator that point in the direction of assigning preponderant blame for the nascent tragedy to Jérôme. To face the reader at every point with conflicting motivations, to confuse his sense of direction while at the same time surreptitiously pointing toward the north, Gide has found the appropriate form. To make the reader in a sense the accomplice of his "flabby" hero in his blindness and in his insensitivity, the devices of the frequently obtuse Narrator, of Alissa's unexpected diary, are well chosen.

Much has been made of the religious symbolism in this novel that is overtly suggested by the quoted Bible verses. For example, Jérôme's seeing the door to Alissa's room as the *narrow gate,* a kind of *press* through which he must pass with effort. However, when

the true role of Jérôme has been penetrated more deeply, the possibility of a Freudian symbolism becomes even more likely than
that of a purely Christian symbolism. For Jérôme, the possibility of
a movement toward sexual fulfillment seems indeed painful, an
almost impossible goal demanding great effort. That he specifically
connects the symbol with the door to Alissa's bedroom could well
be significant.

The importance of these symbols in giving a "timeless dimension"
to the novel has been pointed out (Brée, p. 158). It now seems possible to see in them an aid to uncovering a more specific truth. The
symbol of the garden reappears constantly. So charming, warm, and
inviting in the early descriptions, the garden (as Miss Brée suggests)
seems definitely hostile to Jérôme when he returns there for his final
meeting with Alissa. The dog barks at him. There is a new gate and
a new gardener. The garden is still Alissa's, but it is as though
Jérôme no longer has a right to be there. But it is not so much that
the two lovers can not move beyond the garden's confines (as Miss
Brée also suggests); it is rather that, because Jérôme has failed to
cultivate the garden, it no longer responds to him. He has left it
fallow, so he is finally shut out, finally shut out of the place where
he had been so welcome, of the life that had tendered toward him
its every passion.

If *La Porte étroite* does not have universal appeal, it may well be
in part because it has little movement. It is static (see Brée, p. 159),
but precisely because it had to be, because the character that
Jérôme had to be stifled all normal movement. This substantive
reality is admirably reflected in the tempo that Gide has given to
the work. All progression is either illusory or artificial. We remain
at the static point of Jérôme's arrested development. It is not the
"restraint and purity of line" that Gide has given to the work that
has eliminated "spontaneity and richness" in the characters as has
been suggested (see Brée, p. 158). It is the inescapable fact that
Jérôme could not be what he was not that banishes spontaneity,
not only from the action, but from the style—but only from the
style of the parts having to do with Jérôme himself. Spontaneity
has not been banished from the letters of Alissa and from her
diary in spite of all Jérôme's influence to the contrary. Tragically,
there was, however, a forced suppression of her spontaneity in her
face to face relationships with her cousin. Perhaps the reason that
Gide did not like the parts he wrote for Jérôme (*Journal I*, p. 276,
Sunday, 7 November 1909) is that he somehow felt his own sup-

pressed guilt too clearly reflected in him. If the style of all parts of
the *récit* that proceed from Jérôme is dull, it represents a dull, obtuse side of himself which he detested and which he could only
bring himself to recognize fully and overtly forty-three years later
in *Et nunc manet in te*. His fundamental, almost unconscious
honesty, not to mention his artistic integrity, somehow forced him
to project a truer light on a story that had been a more simply conceived criticism of a certain mystical tendency. This dual and contradictory inspiration of *La Porte étroite* is reflected not only in the
tortuous meanderings of its story line, but also, and just as basically,
in the fundamental differences in tone, rhythm, and tempo between
the two stylistic registers, that of Jérôme and that of Alissa.

The key to the understanding of the direction of the novel (which
is neither single nor simple) lies in the rejection of the "tragedy of
renunciation" interpretation in favor of that of resignation born of
loss of hope. Need we point out that *renunciation* and *resignation*
are not the same?

La Porte étroite must be seen to be a confession almost as much
as *Si le grain ne meurt* or *Et nunc manet in te*—a confession whose
most important element is expressed through the character of
Jérôme rather than in the more obvious mystical tendency which
Alissa may give the appearance of incarnating. To confess more
openly than he did would have been detrimental to the plot line,
for the impression of Jérôme's blindness had of necessity to be
maintained. Just as in *L'Immoraliste*, the Narrator's main problem
is reflected in his "thoughtlessness" and "blindness." Rather than
balancing each other's excesses, *La Porte étroite* and *L'Immoraliste*
are in reality two manifestations of the same problem.

Jérôme kills Alissa just as surely as Michel kills Marceline in
L'Immoraliste.

The Counterfeiters

by Germaine Brée

The combats of truth and error is eating of the Tree of Life.
—William Blake, *The Marriage of Heaven and Hell*

The *Journal of the Counterfeiters* is neither a guide to Gide's novel nor an explanation of it. At most, it can raise certain questions in the reader's mind concerning Gide's intentions, the merits of the techniques he used, and the scope of the book itself. On the whole, it stresses those characteristics of fiction which Gide wanted to do away with: descriptions in the realistic manner, a plot around which to drape his story, motivational analysis explaining the characters' behavior, the kind of narration so smoothly organized that it carries the reader along on a kind of conveyer belt, and the traditional sort of conclusion.

Yet all these customary habitual ingredients have a place in *The Counterfeiters*. Gide provides a geographic and social setting, a main plot, and several subordinate plots. The succession of events is carefully timed and the novel is brought to a conclusion by means of two, perhaps even three, successive denouements, the first two partially happy endings, the third tragic.[1] All the energies set in motion in the first part of the novel come to a temporary rest at the end, an equilibrium on which the book closes.[2]

"The Counterfeiters." From *Gide*, by Germaine Breé (New Brunswick, N. J.: Rutgers University Press, 1963), pp. 230–50. Copyright © 1963 by Rutgers State University. Reprinted by permission of The Rutgers University Press.

[1] Bernard returns home, intellectually matured; Olivier, in Edouard's charge, has rejected the enticement of the literary counterfeiter Passavant; Boris is dead.

[2] As in *Lafcadio's Adventures* Gide wanted his novel to give the impression that it could be continued. It is true that, having come through the particular set of events recounted in *The Counterfeiters*, the characters are ready to go on living, as in life itself. The book closes with Edouard's remark concerning his interest in Caloub, Bernard's young brother, a rather impertinent and not really necessary fillip at the end to stress the continuation of life. But the particular

Gide situates his story carefully: in the Luxembourg section of Paris and in Saas-Fée, Switzerland—a narrow geographic area but with ramifications in France, England, Corsica, Poland, America, and Africa. The effect is of a small brilliantly lighted stage beyond which the entire world extends. Lady Griffith's America, the Africa of Vincent, the Poland of La Pérouse's son are the faraway frontiers of a region in which even Pau, in southern France, is considered a place of exile. The setting of *The Counterfeiters* resembles the universe of the ancients: a small flat space surrounded by the vague masses of mythical continents. Gide had wanted the setting of his novel to be "saturated with myth," his Luxembourg Gardens to be as imaginary as Shakespeare's Forest of Arden in *As You Like It*. Actually one may feel rather constrained by the naïveté and narrowness of the Gidian perspective. The borders of the known world in *The Counterfeiters* are rather quickly reached.

The small coherent group of characters belong to a part of the respectable Parisian bourgeoisie, shut in upon itself and limited in its contacts. The foreigners who happen to intrude are promptly thrown out: little Boris, from Poland, commits suicide and Lady Griffith is assassinated by Vincent.

The Protestant milieu, as always, furnishes the main contingent of characters, the family of the Vedel-Azaïs, the Moliniers and the novelist Edouard; but a variety of so-called Protestant righteousness even hangs over the Catholic Profitendieus.[3] Gide did not wish to raise the denominational issue as he had done in *Strait Is the Gate*. What the four families most actively involved in his story have in common is their connection with liberal professions: they are magistrates, professors, pastors, writers. On the fringes, the aristocratic Passavants and the politically inclined Adamantis suggest further upper-middle class connections. Quite late in the story there appears a character who seems out of place in such a respectable group, the counterfeiter Strouvilhou. The social setting, like the geographic, stretches farther than is at first apparent. What shuts the characters in is their own limited point of view, whereas in truth they are "imbricated," as Gide would say, in an apparently unlimited social world.

---

events with which the novel is concerned have spun out their course by its conclusion.

[3] Gide sometimes unblushingly puns when giving his characters their names: Profitendieu = Prospers-in-God; Passavant = Gets there first.

Gide may have had trouble initially in attaching his heroes to definite families and "relating" them to each other. Nevertheless, he did so with the greatest care, although he leaves it to his reader to spell out the relations that operate implicitly through the story. M. Profitendieu and M. Molinier are magistrates. The wealthier Profitendieus have four children of whom only one, the illegitimate son Bernard, plays a part in the novel. Gide winds the main threads of his plot around the three sons of the Moliniers: Vincent, Olivier, and Georges. The Vedel-Azaïs family, educators and pastors, people the novel with their five children: Rachel, Laure, Sarah, Alexandre and Armand. Boris, the grandson of the music teacher, La Pérouse, attends the Azaïs school as does the nephew of Strouvilhou, Ghéridanisol. All the characters are thus interconnected in a thousand ways and from generation to generation. Gide stresses the continuity within which the opposition of the generations will operate. The friendship of Olivier and Bernard is echoed in the mutual esteem of their fathers. Ghéridanisol goes to the Azaïs school because his uncle went there before him. The web of connections stretches backward in time, giving the story temporal dimensions rather than the more traditional spatial ones.

At the center of the web is Edouard, Mme. Molinier's half brother. He is connected to the Vedel-Azaïs family through his halfhearted love affair with Laure and by having boarded in their school, where he met Strouvilhou and had La Pérouse as his music teacher. He knows Count Passavant, who is one of his literary colleagues, and he will greatly influence Bernard and Olivier. All the events of the novel, in some way, direct or indirect, move within Edouard's orbit. Incidental characters cross his path, wending their way in and out of the main stream of the story, suggesting further perspectives that Edouard's limited attention cannot encompass.

The fabric of the novel is not pieced together to fit the dimensions of the story; the story, Gide implies, stretches beyond his novel in space, time, and human connections. The characters fall into two main groups: the parents and grandparents; the younger generation, all under forty. Edouard, who is just thirty-six when the story begins, moves between the two groups. The conflict between the generations and yet the continuity of the heritage that binds them together is an integral theme.

The young group initiates the action, their parents being immobilized in a sort of social and mental status quo. Some of the lively characters under forty are young adults, already "committed," engaged in life—Edouard, Count Passavant, Vincent, Rachel, and Laure. Others—Bernard, Olivier, Armand, and their friends, all around eighteen—are uncertainly poised between their dependence as schoolboys and their passage into adult life. The baccalaureate, the terminal high-school examination in France, symbolizes this transition, which is one of the major themes in the novel. The younger teen-agers—Georges, Boris, Ghéridanisol, and Phiphi—are at the difficult stage between childhood and adolescence. As the novel progresses, the spotlight moves from group to group, concentrating sometimes on one and sometimes on the other. But whether they are at the center of the stage or in the wings, all the characters are present and active in the novel from the very beginning.

When the story begins one intrigue, involving Edouard, Vincent, Laure, and her husband Douviers, is coming to its end; a second involving Bernard, Olivier, Edouard and Passavant is shaping up; a third is vaguely suggested: the illegal, clandestine activity of the high-school boys which preoccupies the two magistrates. It will emerge fully only in the third part of the book.

The characters are tied to their milieu and few break away. When Bernard Profitendieu decides to be adventurous and break with his family, he does nothing more hazardous than to become secretary to Edouard, the uncle of his closest friend, Olivier, and then subsequently to find a job at the Azaïs boarding school. Laure Vedel, in love with Edouard, ventures as far as Pau, only to be seduced there by Edouard's oldest nephew, Vincent.

The professional ambitions of the characters are equally limited. The most arduous profession these young men envisage is literary journalism; the most violent political commitment, joining a right-wing party. Aside from usual and less usual love affairs, the main cause of excitement is the launching of an avant-garde review; the most fascinating adventure of the year is a literary dinner; and the greatest trial is the baccalaureate. Even the reprehensible activities of the boys, which so gravely concern the two magistrates, are cut to scale. They are merely those of a group of schoolboys, cynically indulging with prostitutes in their first sexual experiences.

The rare "explorers" like Vincent Molinier and Alexandre Vedel, who take off for darkest Africa, are deliberately relegated to the periphery of the novel. They come to a bad end or disappear in those obscure regions that extend beyond the boundaries of Gide's stage. The small world Gide chose to depict has nothing very glorious to recommend it. It is ethically and socially refined almost to the point of effeteness.[4] Yet it has the characteristic traits of the well-to-do and well-meaning upper-middle class in Western Europe, as it was before the series of brutal wars which disrupted its righteous tranquillity.

Gide's approach to this world may seem surprising, but the people with whom he deals are quite recognizably related to those also depicted in novels as different from Gide's as Proust's and Martin du Gard's. Galsworthy and Meredith treat their English counterparts and Mann describes their German equivalents in those "people of the plain" whom Hans Castorp rejects in *The Magic Mountain*. Gide merely eliminated from his story all economic or social considerations. His characters interest him only in so far as they are connected with the self-appointed guardians of the ethical values in their society, those values embodied in the law, the church and the educational system.

Nothing in *The Counterfeiters* suggests that the earth is not peopled entirely by persons of this type, and this is perhaps a weakness. Rare are the novels with characters so far removed from the concerns of average human beings. Toward the end of the novel, as Bernard hesitates at a sort of crossroads in his life, Gide imagines that an angel takes him by the hand and leads him "into the poor sections of the town, whose wretchedness Bernard had never suspected. Evening was falling. They wandered for a long time among tall, sordid houses, inhabited by disease, prostitution, shame, crime, and hunger." [5] Bernard's angel turns aside to weep, but the reader is tempted rather to shrug his shoulders. It is all too obvious that for Gide the "sordid crimes" perpetrated by the poor are not of the same kind as the more elegantly reprehensible activities of his young heroes.

Gide's human world, in spite of his good will, was limited. The only dramas that flourish in this milieu are the casual, carefully concealed complications of adultery. At worst, the pious pastor Vedel is inwardly tormented because of his addiction to masturbation, to which he alludes in secret code in his journal. The taboo concerning sex is total and on the whole Freud is still almost unknown in the fictional universe described. Yet Gide's characters are

---

[4] The actual activities of Gide's gang, increasingly dangerous though they tend to become, seem relatively harmless compared to the widespread battles of teenage urban gangs since World War II. Nonetheless, Gide raises most pertinently the whole question of adolescent delinquency.

[5] *Les Faux-Monnayeurs, Oeuvres Complètes*, XII, 489.

all involved in a web of trite clandestine love-affairs which keep them on the go: Laure's adultery; Vincent's liaisons; the brief encounter of the two adolescents, Bernard and Sarah; Edouard's and Passavant's seduction of Olivier. Edouard, attracted by Olivier, forgets his love for Laure. Laure, disappointed with Edouard, marries Douviers and has a liaison with Vincent. Vincent abandons Laure for Lady Griffith. Bernard leaves home when he discovers he is illegitimate. Armand contracts syphilis in some sordid adventure.

The love affairs are handled casually. Sex plays a role in all these lives, but it is a role neither glamorous nor mysterious. Fortunately Gide does not intend to make it a source of romance; otherwise his novel might have foundered in the embarrassing honeyed sweetness of Edouard's love for Olivier. Sex in *The Counterfeiters* merely opens the way for more disruptive, dangerous and perturbing forces. It sets the characters in motion and its omnipresence suggests that all, in some vital fashion, are governed by its exigencies.

This undercover sexual activity, general though it is, is carefully concealed by everyone. The children would never guess that their parents had ever yielded to erotic impulses were there not to inform them of what goes on behind the scenes the secret letters and locked drawers dear to eighteenth-century fiction which quite naturally find their place in Gide's novel. The parents, in turn, pretend not to notice the love affairs of their children: Oscar Molinier, for example, dwells at some length on the edifying aspects of his two sons' most questionable friendships. Only at the end does Olivier's mother admit the truth concerning her son's homosexual affair, an indirect and reluctant admission.

The clandestine activities of Georges Molinier and his teenage gang are more brutal. They involve not only current concepts of morality but also the law, and they culminate in what is in fact a murder. Gide used to advantage the insights he had gained into adolescent crime when he was a member of the jury in the Assize Court of Rouen. The gang psychology and brutality of his teenagers are depicted clearly and forcefully. At the beginning of the novel M. Molinier and M. Profitendieu, we learn, are concerned about a vice ring which M. Profitendieu is investigating, which he now knows implicates schoolboys with respectable backgrounds. These are no longer the "scissor thieves" of *The Immoralist,* the picturesque little Arabs whose exoticism accounts for their untoward actions. But the investigators whose job it is to detect crime and make it inoperative cannot tolerate the thought that it has infected their own social class. Silence is preferable to truth. Like the illicit sexual relationships of their elders, the teenagers' antisocial activities are hushed up.

While the love intrigues in *The Counterfeiters* give the novel its picaresque atmosphere, the hidden criminal activity is a source of mystery. The reader, rather like Profitendieu, the investigating magistrate, comes upon certain clues and coincidences and begins to glimpse a rather alarming reality beneath the quiet surface of the story, as Strouvilhou and a counterfeit coin make their simultaneous entrance toward the middle of the book. The mystery attached to both, at first intriguing to the reader, soon becomes sinister. A menace hangs over Gide's pleasant and insignificant set of characters, so full of good will and so self-absorbed. Georges Molinier's trail leads to the mysterious Strouvilhou, but so do many others. As soon as he puts in an appearance it becomes clear that Strouvilhou's influence is all-pervasive, that Gide's whole cast of characters is connected with him. They are all prevaricators and, to varying degrees, counterfeiters. All proffer their false coins in the hope that they will be accepted as real, or at least that no detective will appear to investigate their origin.

This is the heart of the novel. Gide's characters and their concerns may seem insignificant. The narrative tone, rapid, detached and slightly mocking, emphasizes the picaresque quality of the story. But the real subject Gide is handling is neither commonplace nor slight. It brings to light a deep-seated equivocation governing the relationships in the group, exemplified in the acts of all the characters.

"The combats of truth and error," wrote Blake, "is eating of the Tree of Life." Eating of the Tree of Life is what Gide's adolescents do, as their parents have done before them. But nothing prepares them for the flavor of the fruits they taste. Of their educators one could say with Blake:

> They take the two contraries which are called qualities, with which
> Every substance is clothed. They name them good and evil.
> From them they make an abstract which is a negation
> Not only of the substance from which it is derived
> A murderer of its own body, but also a murderer
> Of every Divine Member.[6]

[6] *Poems of William Blake,* ed. by W. B. Yeats (London: The Muses Library), pp. 231, 255.

Wherever they turn the youngsters find good and evil inextricably mixed, yet their elders righteously proclaim that good alone reigns around them.

In contrast, Gide's novel is conceived to bring out a deeper pattern and truth as Gide sees it. The intrigues of the counterfeiters notwithstanding, the "combats of truth and error" are fought in the novel on all levels by each character. They give the story the hidden epic value with which Gide strove to suffuse his tale.

Each character follows his own path, journeying through temptations and dangers. Bernard is a winner in this contest, but the novel is strewn with those who are defeated, temporarily or permanently; those who wander around aimlessly; and those who, somewhere along the way, were taken captive or joined the wrong faction. There is a kind of "pilgrim's progress" involved, particularly for the adolescents. Their struggles at this level take place in solitude. Social institutions, family, justice, schools, religion all league together to maintain the righteous fiction of social and moral order. The love affairs secretly weld individuals to one another in a conspiracy of silence. The teen-age delinquents band together to challenge the restraints imposed upon them. The counterfeiters are linked together by their defiance of the law. But nothing binds the Gidian pilgrims to anyone else. Entangled as they are, they can either accept the struggle between truth and error or join the ranks of the counterfeiters, thus alienating themselves from the "substance" of life.

At different levels, therefore, Gide's characters go through solitary trials and adventures through which they are led to an active organic participation in the fight with or against the counterfeiters. In these encounters their spiritual solitude gives them a freedom untrammeled by the tight social bonds which link them to each other. This freedom, the empty space that surrounds each one, is a device whereby Gide emphasizes the inner quality that determines their respective orientations.

At one point Bernard says that he would like his life "to ring true, with a pure, authentic sound." Gide has endowed each character with his own sound. The most serious source of counterfeit is the attempt, whether individual or social, to reduce all dissonance in favor of that universal and wholly theoretical perfect and continuous chord which haunts the imagination of the old piano teacher, La Pérouse. For the sake of some form of harmony all the characters in the novel, at times and more or less deliberately, indulge in counterfeit. The theme is taken up in turn by each instrument in Gide's human orchestra.

Certain characters are centers of emission of the false coin; in varying degrees what they put forth can be deceptive and dangerous. Passavant is a counterfeiter from vanity, from the need to cut a figure in the world: through counterfeit literary pursuits, counterfeit sentiments, and a counterfeit wit. He deals in small coin and deceives no one except, temporarily, young Olivier. The Englishwoman, Lady Griffith, more dangerous, perverts Vincent, a promising young doctor, to the extent that Gide eventually throws him out of the novel, literally "to the devil." At the very end of the story we learn that Vincent, by this time having killed Lady Griffith, has gone mad and thinks he is the devil in person—a very moral ending. The sense of his adventure is pointed up in the well-known anecdote told by Lady Griffith at the beginning of the novel. Once shipwrecked, Lady Griffith, herself safely hauled into one of the lifeboats, saw the sailors cut off the hands of those unlucky survivors who tried to clamber on after the boat had been filled to capacity. Since then luck and an unscrupulous ferocity had appeared to her perversely romantic eyes to be the only safe guiding principles in life. In a few quick stages she teaches Vincent to gamble on his luck and to cut off all restraining hands, Laure's the first among them. Vincent's unbridled commitment to his appetite is self-destructive, but destroys him alone, not others. Vincent is not, as he thinks, the devil but merely one of the devil's victims.

The master "counterfeiter" and his mint are a good deal more dangerous: pious old Azaïs and his establishment. Strouvilhou, the real-life counterfeiter, is only one of its by-products. All the major characters in the book wander through the precincts of the school. It is the Vatican of the novel. Just as Profitendieu, on the trail of crime, is gradually led back to Strouvilhou, so the story inevitably leads to the school where the major plot is hatched that brings about the one irreparable event, the death of young Boris. There in his study old Azaïs reigns as though he were God. Azaïs, himself, has a certain pleasing innocence that "rings true." But everyone around him must echo back to him his own sound. Systematically he acknowledges only the purest good around him, every day casting the serpent out of Paradise. He is an unbearable burden upon his family and students, who are forced to conceal or overlook all that does not jibe with Pastor Azaïs's "perfect chord." Their only resort is lying, and prevarication teems around the old gentleman. The insigne that young Georges wears in his buttonhole, the insigne of his teen-age gang, becomes in Azaïs's eyes the emblem of an association for moral improvement. All his children live under the shadow of guilt, unable to grapple with the ambivalence in their own motivations and impulses. In the Azaïs boarding school, the combats of truth and error are impossible. Evil thrives unchallenged, and Strouvilhou has no trouble recruiting his accomplices there.

Strouvilhou is the natural complement of the old headmaster. He is bitterly aware of the illusory nature of Azaïs's idyllic view of things. A nihilist, he sees only the lie beneath the façade and, revolted, openly declares war on the lie. He has become a perverter out of a disappointed idealism akin to Azaïs's own. Detecting everywhere only the counterfeit, he cynically decides to live on it. Morally speaking, the other characters fall somewhere between Azaïs and Strouvilhou. On the headmaster's side there is society, the myth of harmonious family life, the myth of childish innocence, the myth of punishment and reward, and the myth of parental infallibility—every counterfeit that can help put up a decorous screen between people and the plain truth they all know. On Strouvilhou's side there are the young people, apparently cynical but actually counterfeiters only because of ignorance, bafflement or distress.

Bernard becomes a counterfeiter when he discovers the large crack behind the family façade of perfect respectability. Georges and Phiphi at fourteen become counterfeiters because no other outlet is offered for their violent and unrecognized physical energies. Armand becomes a counterfeiter out of despair, unable to live up to his pious family's exigencies. Boris becomes a counterfeiter out of his great desire for purity and the intimate distress caused by the sense of his own unworthiness.[7] Edouard is a counterfeiter because he cannot face such brutal realities as Boris's death, preferring to bypass them in his novel as in his life. Wherever fiction takes the place of truth, counterfeit coin starts to circulate. Like Edouard, the counterfeiters are bad novelists, peddling their ersatz substitutes for truth.

Azaïs and Strouvilhou both judge on appearances, hence the confusion they generate. "Go," said Blake, "put off holiness and put on intellect." [8] That is just what Gide, humorously, proposes we do. Intelligence regulates the play of light and shadow in the novel,

---

[7] Dr. Delay goes in detail into the connection between Boris's excruciating struggle against masturbation and the shattering experence Gide went through as a child when he was publicly called to task for just the same thing, then temporarily expelled from his school [Jean Delay, *La Jeunesse d'André Gide*, I, 253–57].
[8] *Poems of William Blake*, XXXIV.

suffusing it with a slightly ironic, nondogmatic form of intelligence. The perceptive moralist in Gide lent a hand to the artist. There may have been in Gide himself a Strouvilhou and, even more, an Azaïs, an Edouard, and a Passavant, but in *The Counterfeiters* he succeeded in keeping them at a distance. The humor which pervades the book gives his characters an autonomous yet recognizably human flavor. Semiallegorical, semireal, they disconcert the dogmatic moralist in Gide's readers, far more prone than he was to reduce novels to reassuring parables. To distinguish truth from error requires a perspicacity incessantly alert to the thousand snares laid by gullibility.

There are no general conclusions to be drawn from any individual situation in *The Counterfeiters,* no ready-made roles to be assumed. At the beginning of the novel Vincent tells Lady Griffith about the surprising discoveries concerning the organism of deep-sea fish. They had been thought to be blind, but it was found that almost all had eyes. "Why eyes with no means of seeing? . . . And at last it was discovered that each of these creatures which people first insisted were creatures of darkness, gives forth and projects before and around it its *own* light." [9] Bernard is a character who learns to trust his own light. But no conclusion can be drawn as to what Olivier should do, for to his fish story Vincent adds another. Each species of ocean fish subsists only in waters containing certain solutions of salt, varying with the species. They move in layers. When an individual fish moves too far up or too far down, it weakens and becomes easy prey for alien fish. To each, therefore, his own dosage of good and evil. [10] Gide's symbol thus accommodates an inexhaustible number of connected images and themes with many variations.

The reading of the novel itself is something of an adventure, so finely meshed are the wheels which regulate its movement. Wherever possible, Gide used the present tense for his narrative, as he had in *Lafacadio's Adventures,* to emphasize his departure from the traditional "story told in retrospect" that relies on various combinations of past tenses. The narrator's comments along the way are calculated to give the impression that things are actually developing as the novel advances. And yet, somewhat as in a movie,

[9] Gide. *Oeuvres Complètes* (Paris, 1932–39), XII, 223.
[10] Passavant notes the "pun," from which Gide drew ample suggestions. In French slang a person who is "déssalé," or "unsalted," is cynically sophisticated. Vincent, one might say, "went off the deep end" or "got into deep water" far too "salty" for him.

they take place in a different world, submitting to different necessities and rhythms. No single point of view directs the narrative. The narrator, whom one naturally first identifies with the author, starts to tell the story. Almost immediately he turns it over to Bernard and thenceforward the point of view travels back and forth as characters move in and out of the scene. Gide handles these shifts in perspective with great smoothness, relying mainly on a rapid, conversational tone to give the story an easy, uninterrupted flow. But the narration projects light only on the narrow segment of the action that each character perceives. No one, not even the unidentified first narrator himself, sees the complete sweep of circumstance relating to each event.

Bernard runs away from home, steals a suitcase, and by chance gets a job as Edouard's secretary; Vincent wins heavily at roulette, abandons Laure and becomes Lady Griffith's lover; Edouard comes back from London, collects Laure and also Bernard, and promises old La Pérouse to bring his grandson, Boris, back to Paris. Olivier meets Passavant and becomes editor of an avant-garde review. Old La Pérouse resolves to commit suicide on a given day: all this occurs within thirty hours or so between a certain Wednesday afternoon in late June and the following Thursday night. But Bernard uncovers a set of old letters, and reads and so does the reader with him —Edouard's *Journal*—so that along the way the reader acquires a sense of continuity and pattern that the characters lack.

Within the novel paths crisscross unexpectedly. The characters, like balls on a narrow billiard table, bump against each other, deflecting each other, continually diverting each other from their original paths. Bernard's intrusion into Edouard's life is just such an unforeseeable diversion. The successive diversions caused by such impacts seem to scatter the balls at random. But from diversion to diversion they finally bring about the culminating event in the novel, Boris's death.

All the events noted in Edouard's *Journal,* which Bernard discovers, touch upon Laure's wedding nine months previously, and mesh in with the random set of events which take place in June. Laure, pregnant and abandoned by Vincent, calls Edouard back to Paris. He is attracted by Olivier but lets himself be persuaded rather to take Bernard as his secretary. Not knowing what to do with himself, he decides, on the spur of the moment, to go and get Boris in Saas-Fée. On his return his real inner concern reasserts itself, he becomes engrossed in Olivier's concerns.

But, as a rebound of all these movements, young Boris meanwhile has been transferred to the Azaïs school. As he arrives there and the third part of the story begins, all the apparently unrelated threads of the action come together, and all the characters, including Azaïs and Strouvilhou. No single character sees what is taking place, though all have their part in it. Gide's deconcentrated plot has a significance and an invisible line of progression reflects his intent. In the third part of the story all the "diversions" are rapidly dealt with. The only love story that really interested Gide, Edouard and Olivier's, ends happily after the latter's attempted suicide. Bernard, like the prodigal son, is on his way back home, and Laure on her way to her husband, Douviers. Armand has joined the counterfeiters. The Azaïs school is quite prosperous. Frightened by the message Edouard relays from Profitendieu, the schoolboy gang seems to have stopped its profitable dealings in counterfeit coins. La Pérouse and his grandson are reunited. All is for the best in the best of all possible worlds.

The schoolboys' secret society of "strong men" now takes the center of the stage. The first suicide victim, Boris, is picked in a fake drawing of lots. The fast-moving tempo suddenly halts as the whole novel plunges into a nightmarish reality. While all the main characters have been absorbed in their own lives, the novel itself, operating in a large framework comprising these individual lives, has been leading up to this single shocking event. Boris's fate develops in the shadow cast by the errors and blindness of the others. When he steps forward in front of his grandfather's desk into the chalk circle prepared by the gang and raises the pistol to his forehead, suddenly, in retrospect, all the characters and actions in the novel appear trivial and singularly irresponsible. Like Lafcadio's tossing Fleurissoire off the train, Boris's death changes the perspectives on the whole story.

Boris is the victim of the counterfeiters. Edouard, when he learns of Boris's death, waves it aside as too brutal for his novel, with a few righteous remarks on how inopportune it was for the poor Vedel-Azaïs family, just as he had waved aside the false coin Bernard had brought to his attention. But so far as Gide is concerned, the counterfeit coin and the schoolboy suicide are the very substance of his novel, its central inner core. A glance backward over the story reveals all the responsibilities at work in Boris's death. Edouard is easily the most responsible. But had Bernard, to whom Boris is entrusted, been less concerned with himself; had La Pérouse not loaded the pistol; had Profitendieu really done his job; had

Azaïs, enamoured with his image of innocent childhood, not emboldened the gang; had the psychiatrist to whom Boris had been entrusted not put Boris's secret into Strouvilhou's hands; had his little friend Bronja not died . . .

Gide planned his novel so that it might approximate his view of how a great many events come about, *not* through a straight, relatively simple interplay of chance, situation, and motivation. An event such as the death of Boris combines innumerable chance factors and, in each, a share of human weakness. Boris's fate is not the consequence of any one set of circumstances. It is made possible by the conjunction of several disparate and random series of activities. All the events in the first part of the novel create a pattern of relationships among the characters. But these are not fixed constellations, each character proceeds along his own path. Edouard's *Journal* is not a Proustian plunge into the past. It is a fictional device which allows Gide to enlarge the temporal dimensions of the novel, so that he can plot trajectories in time, orientations which determine new patterns, and future dispersions. Certainly this is the most original part of *The Counterfeiters* and by far the most arresting.

The novel, which begins at an almost frenzied pace, seems to bog down during Edouard's stay at Saas-Fée, and then to break up at random into a series of secondary plots, connected only by one moral theme—the theme of counterfeit. Only at the very end does Gide's scheme become clear. He wanted his novel to be an "imitation" of an action in the manner of a classical play, revealing all the forces, whether visible or not, which determine an act like Boris's: chance, circumstance, motivation, atmosphere, error working through human contacts, intentions, failures. All the events and characters are seen in relation to that act, so that the whole may realize the "erosion of contours" Gide wanted to obtain.

The Counterfeiters has the free lines, the abstract planes, the multiplication of perspectives, the interplay of form and idea, as well as the humor characteristic of the soties. But unlike the soties, Gide's novel treats characters who are not mere pawns, and it has a serious, human significance. *The Counterfeiters* seems to convey something life had disclosed to Gide, who is not Edouard.

The second part of the novel, which takes place in the Alpine Saas-Fée, introduces an interval of repose in the story. But Gide's "infernal machine" is in the background all wound up and set for the dénouements. Meanwhile Edouard, Laure, and Bernard discuss Edouard's novel and Boris's cure with Sophroniska, the psychoanalyst. Strouvilhou passes through leaving behind the counterfeit gold piece Bernard finds in a shop and takes to Edouard. At this point the theme of counterfeit coin brings up a more basic problem, the paradox of its resemblance to real coin. When the action again moves forward, in line with Gidian dialectics, truth has become the main concern, not counterfeit. As always during the interval of repose, Gide clarifies and intellectualizes his theme. Sophroniska deals with the same problems as Profitendieu in his criminal investigation, but in the realm of individual psychology. Boris, with his "Yes-No" answers and his nervous furies, shows clear evidences of deep disorder. Observing the symptoms, Sophroniska patiently attempts to track down the hidden ill, to dislodge it, and to free Boris from its grip. Edouard suggests, and subsequent events tend to corroborate his opinion, that Boris's trouble, if mercilessly tracked down, will only change its aspect and take root more deeply in less accessible parts of his psyche. In the same way, when Profitendieu shuts up the house where the schoolboy orgies are held, the boys turn to peddling counterfeit money. Warned by Profitendieu that their activities are known to the police, they turn to sadism and organize a kind of "superman club." Unhappily, Sophroniska has prepared a ready victim for them.

Boris suffers terrible feelings of guilt for indulging in what he calls the "magic" which relieves him of his solitude, and which he somehow connects with a certain talisman. Believing that good always triumphs, Sophroniska attempts to circumvent evil by eliminating it. She takes away Boris's talisman, but makes the error of handing it over to Strouvilhou, who in turn gives it to the schoolboys. Newly enrolled at the Azaïs school, Boris joins their gang, wistfully wanting to be accepted as one of the boys, wistfully anxious to harbor no suspicion of evil intent in their advances. And yet he is well aware that all is not as they describe it to him. Boris's enemy lurks in recesses well out of Sophroniska's reach, in the person of Ghéridanisol, who does evil for the sake of evil. Boris, unprepared for battle, is totally defenseless.

Meanwhile, cozy in his own comfortable realm, the literary Edouard toys with the word "pure." He plagiarizes Gide, imagining a novel whose hero, a novelist, writes the story of the genesis of a novel. Its theme is to be the struggle between reality as observed and the novelist's idea of the nature of that reality. Edouard reads two pages of his book—a kind of parody of *Fruits of the Earth*—to Georges, in the hope of influencing him. He fails completely.

Edouard is not Gide's spokesman but, like other of the characters, he introduces those variations on Gide's main themes that apply to his particular profession as novelist. Edouard moves to the periphery of the action as events converge toward the central catastrophe. He ends up as a sort of supernumerary. The range of his vision falls short of the requirements of his art. He wants reality to "ring" exclusively according to a "chord" of his own choosing.

Gide's *Counterfeiters* is a novel of adolescence, a novel of orientation which depicts young people emerging from various forms of myth into the reality of life. For the first time Gide's work has really deep social implications. He portrays the struggle of the young to discover through trial and error the genuine forces and limits of their personalities, in the face of obsolete social forms and ethics which tend to impose stereotyped feelings and attitudes upon them. Experience teaches Edouard nothing, since he ignores it, whereas Georges, shaken by Boris's death, alters his disastrous course. For Gide, to live, as to write a novel, is to undergo the test of reality.

By the time he wrote *The Counterfeiters* Gide had left behind him the ironic, critical novel. For his young people the "trial by life" ends with a return to their own social orbit. From error to authenticity, the way is difficult but open. Each separate adventure in the novel, as well as the novel as a whole, converges toward the discovery of the real and the true as opposed to the false. Bernard gets rid of his silly ideas, while Georges discovers what real monsters lurked behind his revolt. Neither devils nor angels, the characters simply become more human: "As for these antinomies," wrote Gide of devils and angels, "I believe them to be all imaginary . . . but the mere fact of living calls them up, creates them." Gide's novel is oriented away from finding antinomies in life. According to him, life does not long put up with counterfeit. It neither deceives nor disappoints. It is we who disappoint and deceive ourselves:

> In this world: real sufferings; imaginary sufferings. The first can be attenuated; the second almost suppressed. They most often result from a belief in *idols*—or in *bogeymen*. The former are constructions that are venerated and do not deserve to be. The latter are phantoms that are feared and do not deserve to be feared.[11]

Gide felt, as did Proust, that the artist is "prompted" by life but that one of the elements given him is an inner orientation and sensitivity to which he must remain faithful; "it is the secret of the depths

[11] *Journal*, p. 811.

of his flesh that prompts, inspires and decides," he said of the artist. There is really no possible counterfeit in art; there are only individual limitations, success and failure.

The "given elements" of life on which Gide worked are slight, perhaps, but at least they are authentic. The point of view that molded them into a novel, however, is quite broad in scope and original. Gide succeeded in setting up for his story a form which is complex without being arbitrary. It is highly intellectual, yet permeated with a special poetry, made up of humor, lucidity, and that very mystery which springs from "the depths of the flesh." *The Counterfeiters* has neither the power nor the density of Proust's novel or of Joyce's *Ulysses,* its two great contemporaries. The reader can accept it straightforwardly without ever filling in the empty spaces, re-establishing the perspectives, or being moved to laughter by its implicit humor. It will seem outmoded, slight and artificial, and its curious transparency irritating, when the boldness of its structural movement goes unnoticed.

In *The Counterfeiters* Gide overcame his difficulties and facilities as a writer. The antiromantic yet poetic stylization of all the elements of the novel, the orchestration of the diverse voices, the lively pace of the story, the concern with permanent human values, the stringency of the language—all contribute to make *The Counterfeiters* an unusual book. To the ordinary pleasures of novel reading it adds, for the sensitive amateur, the "pure" pleasure of aesthetic understanding. No novel ever written was more "literary" and yet more free of literary influences. What Gide really investigated in his novel is what happens to all forms of "literature," in contact with life. It was perhaps the only real adventure that he himself had fully lived, and as a result, *The Counterfeiters* is the only one of his novels which fully expresses him.

The Consultation

by Jean Delay

> Yet I could not help but worry about my own nature, I mean
> that of my desires . . . I had therefore decided to talk freely
> about it to a doctor.
> —*Et nunc manet in te* [in *Journal* (Pléiade ed.), II], 1130

At the very end of *Si le grain ne meurt* Gide wrote of his engagement to Emmanuèle: "I believed I could give myself to her *completely*,[1] and did so without any reservations." Apparently, at the
time of his engagement he had decided to put an end to that dissociation of pleasure and love which had governed his sexual life until
then. When he married Madeleine "without any reservations," did
he really mean to give up his homosexual habits?

> It was a marriage between heaven and my insatiable hell; but at the
> actual moment, that hell was temporarily suppressed: the tears of my
> mourning had put out all its fires; it was as if I were dazzled by the
> glare of azure, and everything I refused to see had stopped existing
> for me.[2]

Barely two weeks after his mother's death, that celestial glare, that
blinding exaltation, favored an immediate engagement; but as the
emotional intoxication wore off, his usual temptations probably
returned, and with them, some hesitations and doubts as to his

"The Consultation" (original title: "Medical Advice"). From Jean Delay, *The
Youth of André Gide*, translated and abridged by June Guicharnaud. (Chicago:
The University of Chicago Press, 1963), pp. 423–42. Copyright © 1963 by The
University of Chicago Press. First published in *La Jeunesse d'André Gide* (Paris:
Editions Gallimard, 1957), in a slightly extended form. Reprinted by permission
of the author and the publishers.

[1] The italics are mine.
[2] *Si le grain ne meurt*, [in *Journal* (Pléiade edition)], II, 369.

physiological aptitude for marriage. It would be difficult to affirm
that "at the time he married, Gide's illusion about his normalcy was
complete." [3] In October, 1893, he had set out on his travels with
the intention of "normalizing" himself; his first attempts with
Meriem had been successful, but all the others had "pitifully failed,"
whereas his homosexual experiences had been so easy and conclu-
sive that he had believed he had found what was "normal" for him.
Gide was thus faced with a serious problem and was well aware of it,
for he decided to tell a doctor all about his fears.

In *Et nunc manet in te* he wrote about that prenuptial consultation, unmentioned in *Si le grain ne meurt*. He went to see "a rather
well-known specialist," and made a confession that was "as cynical
as possible." The "neurologist" listened to him "smilingly," ex-
amined him, and then drew comforting conclusions:

> And yet you say that you're in love with a young girl; and that you
> hesitate to marry her because, on the other hand, you're aware of
> your tastes. . . . Get married. Get married without fear. And you'll
> quickly realize that all the rest exists only in your imagination. You
> give me the impression of someone who is starved and who up until
> now has tried to subsist on pickles. (I'm accurately quoting his words;
> by heaven, I could hardly forget them!) As soon as you're married,
> you will quickly understand what natural instinct is and will quite
> spontaneously go back to it.[4]

The practitioner who displayed such hardy optimism no doubt believed he was dealing with an emotional and shy young man who
lacked self-confidence, and that all he had to do was to reassure him
good-naturedly. That kind of attitude would have been justified had
Gide been simply anxious and tormented by the fear of sexual inhibition, but the situation was far more complicated and should never
have been treated lightly. We have now come to the point in this
study where an analysis of Gide's sexual problem, as it stood in
1895, seems in order. In a plan for a preface to *Si le grain ne meurt*,
Gide wrote:

> Rousseau says that he wrote his *Confessions* because he believed he
> was unique. I am writing mine for exactly the opposite reasons, and
> because I know that a great many will recognize themselves in them.

[3] Jean Schlumberger, *Madeleine et André Gide*, p. 121.
[4] *Et nunc manet in te*, p. 1130.

—But to what purpose?—I believe that everything that is true can be instructive.[5]

It is precisely because of his intention to tell the truth for representative purposes that it is necessary to reconsider that important question from an angle which has nothing to do with literature.

Given Gide's way of understanding confessions, it is probable that he omitted no detail that might have enlightened the doctor, save that he could not have pointed out a whole group of family circumstances which at that time were considered to have no conection with the sexual question. Moreover, many doctors, even the most learned in the field of nervous illnesses, then knew very little about sexual neuroses. Once they had ascertained that their patient's constitution was normally virile (and Gide's was) and that he had already been capable of heterosexual relations (which was indeed his case), they were of the idea that he had no actual medical problem, as if the doctor could ignore the implications of the mind and the body, or, as they say, the psyche and the soma. The neurologist cannot be personally blamed for his mistake, for it is ascribable to a certain purely somatic conception of medicine, which was far more widespread then than it is today.

Before trying to explain Gide's sexual habits, they must be defined. With regard to his experience in January, 1895, he said: "I now found what was normal for me." What did he mean by "normal" for him? The one word "homosexual" designates "types" that are very different from one another, with one trait in common: the subject and object of desire are of the same sex. "If only, instead of becoming indignant, people would just try to find out what is being talked about. Before discussing, one should always define. Most quarrels further a misunderstanding." [6] In regard to himself, Gide wanted to avoid any possibility of a misunderstanding: he was bent on saying what he was and what he was not. "I call a *pederast* the man who, as the word indicates, falls in love with young boys . . . pederasts, of whom I am one. . . ." [7] He was a pederast or a pedophile—that is, a man whose object of desire is neither man nor woman but the male child or adolescent, at least as long as the

[5] *Oeuvres Complètes*, X, 454.
[6] *Journal*, I, 671.
[7] Ibid.

adolescent remains the *molliter juvenis* spoken of by Pliny. For
Gide, childishness or youthfulness was the condition *sine qua non*
of desirability; mature virility was as horrifying to him as effeminacy.
On that point he hardly ever varied, and the homosexual phantasms
we remarked in *Les Cahiers d'André Walter* and *Le Voyage d'Urien*,
conceived before he had had any experience, were indeed those of
a pedophile. Giving a quite different meaning to certain terms in
medical language, he called a *sodomite* "the man whose desire is
directed to mature men," and an *invert* "the man who, in the
comedy of love, assumes the role of a woman." [8] The author of
Amyntas never hid the fact that he was repelled by one and the
other, and said about the different types of homosexuals: "The
difference between them is so great that they feel profound disgust
for one another." As early as October, 1894, after having read Moll's
book on homosexuality, he wrote:

> He does not differentiate enough between two classes: the effeminate
> men and the others—he constantly mixes them together, and nothing
> is more different, more *contrary*—because one is opposed to the
> other—because for that kind of psychophysiology, that which does not
> attract repels—and each horrifies the other.[9]

Gide was specific about the forms of his homosexual relations.

> We always have great difficulty in understanding the loves of others,
> their way of practicing love. . . . But nothing is more disconcerting
> than the gesture, so different from species to species, by means of
> which each one of them achieves sexual pleasure. . . . It is perhaps,
> on the contrary, in what M. de Gourmont calls "the physics of love"
> that we find the most marked differences not only between man and
> animals but often even from one man to another—to the point that
> were we allowed to watch our neighbor's practices, they would often
> seem as strange, as preposterous, and indeed as monstrous as the
> coupling of batrachians or insects—but why go that far afield? as
> that of dogs and cats. And that is no doubt why the incomprehension
> on this point is so great and the intransigence so ferocious.[10]

He himself was always to remain the André Walter who was "terrified by carnal possession" and as unresponsive to virile aggressivity
as to feminine passivity. As Baudelaire wrote:

[8] Ibid.
[9] Letter to a friend, unpublished.
[10] *Si le grain ne meurt,* pp. 595–96.

There is something in the act of love that is similar to torture or to a surgical operation. . . . Love wants to come out of itself, fuse with its victim like the conqueror with the conquered, and yet keep the conqueror's privileges.[11]

Copulation, whether natural or against nature, provoked a kind of terror in Gide, in that it called to mind a semblance of combat or, to use Baudelaire's expression, the conqueror and the conquered, whatever the assent or the agreement between the partners as to the respective roles they play in the pantomime. In *Si le grain ne meurt* he told about how during one of his trips to Algeria, he was the horrified witness to an act of homosexual fornication between a sodomite and an invert:

He seemed like a huge vampire feeding on a corpse. I could have screamed out with horror. . . . As for me whose only way of taking pleasure is face to face, reciprocally and without violence, and who, like Whitman, am often satisfied by the most furtive contact, I was horrified both by Daniel's way of going about it and by Mohammed's very complacent submission to it.[12]

His homosexual habits were limited to the voluptuous play of his childhood, and differed from it only in that the solitary onanism had become reciprocal onanism with childish partners. Certain of the great writer's self-disparaging remarks, such as: "I shall never be a man, but only a child who has grown old," or: "I'm only a little boy having a good time . . ." do make sense with regard to his sexual behavior, which was to remain infantile.

It seems surprising that Gide, always so careful when it came to distinguishing between pleasure and love, would have picked up the expression cited above, "the physics of love," when he was clearly referring to the physics of pleasure. When he specified that love had played no part in his experience of January, 1895, he was speaking of pleasure for what it was, without mixing in any sentimental or moral considerations, and could not honestly assimilate it to Greek love. But later on, he had Corydon, that Victor Cousin of pedophiles, do just that when he claimed to justify pederasty in the name of the true, the beautiful, and the good. What happened was that in the meanwhile Gide had rationalized his tastes and proceeded to defend them with a whole dialectic, in which so

[11] Charles Baudelaire, *Fusées.*
[12] *Si le grain ne meurt,* pp. 595–96. The allusion is obviously to Walt Whitman.

many sophisms were mixed with valid arguments that a passage
from *Le Journal des Faux-Monnayeurs* could well have been used
as an epigraph for *Corydon*:

> Someone with a so-called false turn of mind? Well! I'll explain it to
> you: it's someone who feels the need of convincing himself that he's
> *right;* someone who uses his reason to serve his instincts, his interests,
> which is worse, or his temperament. . . . He is the first victim of his
> own false reasoning; he ends by convincing himself that he is being
> led by those false reasons.[13]

In any case, Gide's homosexual problem in 1895 was far simpler
and much less involved in sophistries than it was to become later on,
for he had not yet constructed the theory that was meant to justify
his inclinations. The very fact that he went to consult a doctor and
accepted the assurance that he was sexually normal proves that he
was not yet sure that pederasty was "normal" for him.

When he recalled the prenuptial consultation that had put an
end to his hesitations and doubts as to his aptitude for marriage,
Gide added:

> I should have realized at once how very wrong the theorist was.
> He was wrong in the same way as all those who persist in thinking
> that as soon as someone is physiologically normal, his homosexual
> tastes are merely acquired tendencies and can therefore be changed
> with the help of education, promiscuity, and love.[14]

If the first theorist was wrong out of overoptimism, was not the
second wrong out of overfatalism? The passage clearly hints at the
thesis that was to be upheld by the doctrinary Corydon. If one believes homosexuality to be innate, it seems fatal and represents a
destiny; if one believes it to be acquired, it seems modifiable and
represents a choice. The homosexual who claims that his inclinations are "natural" considers them inevitable, thus discouraging be-
forehand any attempt at a struggle and allowing for only one reasonable solution: acceptance, if, of course, he is determined to follow his
"nature" despite all moral or social interdictions. That, we know,
is the viewpoint of Corydon, who invokes Goethe's words:

> Pederasty is as old as humanity itself and we can therefore say that
> it is natural, that it is based upon nature although it goes against

[13] Pp. 58–59.
[14] *Et nunc manet in te,* p. 1130.

nature. What culture has gained, what it has won over nature, should never be allowed to escape; at no price should it be let go.

In other words, Goethe believed that the approbation of heterosexuality and the reprobation of homosexuality represent a cultural victory, but that nature proposes one as well as the other. Corydon, who thinks his habits arc "against custom," not "against nature," is convinced of it, but he is completely opposed to Goethe in the sense that he considers "culture's" gain in that realm unfortunate. Indeed, basing his point of view on a whole documentation borrowed from the history of aesthetics and ethics, sociology and biology, he believes that pederasty, far from being any kind of human inferiority, is a superiority in the scale of values. There is little point in discussing so specious an argument here, for it would lead us far from the problem at hand: was it possible, at the time of the 1895 consultation, to know whether Gide's homosexuality was innate, and therefore fatal, or acquired, and therefore modifiable? Was it, as he proclaimed, inscribed in his nature, or was it, on the contrary, produced by outer influences which turned his instinct from its habitual finality and kept him from reaching maturity? In his *Discours sur l'origine de l'inégalité*, Jean-Jacques Rousseau remarked: "It is no small undertaking to distinguish the native from the artificial in man's present nature." Difficult as it may be, it is still necessary, in tracing the evolution of habits, to distinguish how much is native and how much artificial—that is, how much is constitutional and how much institutional, how much organic and how much environmental.

Gide's physical constitution was normally virile, and we know in another connection that he was not at all incapable of "the impulse that procreates." He apparently had none of the anomalies of the sex characteristics, primary or secondary, which make it possible to consider a hormonal factor at the roots of some homosexuality. Besides, *Corydon* deals only with the pederasty of men who are completely virile biologically, as Gide himself was. Yet modern research in the determination of the "genetic sex" shows that the biological problem is infinitely more complicated than one might have believed. It is possible that any profound and lasting perversion of the sexual instinct implies a constitutional predisposition. Freud himself, who upheld the psychogenesis of the homosexual neurosis, admitted that "without a constitutional predisposition, no neurosis could exist." Be that as it may, the only notable anomaly in Gide's constitution was not of a sexual but of a nervous nature. His temperament was that of someone nervously weak, predisposed to emotional inhibitions and self-doubt, *naturally* shy, exposed to difficulties in social relations and, most particularly, in sexual relations. Many anxious people of that irritable and suggestible temperament might say with Amiel: "Sexuality will have been my Nemesis, my torment since childhood," and invoke "my extraordinary shyness, my embarrassment with women, my violent desires, the fervor of imagination . . . the eternal disproportion between a life of dream and real life, my deadly propensity for detaching myself from the tastes, passions and habits of those of my own age and my own sex . . ." to explain an inhibition, if not a perversion, of which that idiosyncracy can be a predisposing, but not a determining, factor.

When endocrinology discovers nothing abnormal in the distribution of male and female hormones, whose relative preponderance determines the secondary sex characteristics, when the possibility of a biologically characterized inversion or intersexual state is eliminated, the explanation for pederasty must be sought in the psychological history of the development of the instinct. This field of research has largely benefited from psychoanalytical studies. Freud, in his far-reaching analysis of infantile sexuality, has shown that the libido, which is present from the beginnings of life, goes through different stages. At first autoerotic—that is, turned toward itself— it then becomes alloerotic—that is, turned toward an object outside itself. But, at the beginning of the alloerotic stage, it is not unusual for it to direct its energies toward an object of the same sex before directing them toward an object of the opposite sex. Many adolescents who go through a homosexual stage reach the heterosexual stage all the same. But maturity is not complete until both desire and love are concentrated on an object of the opposite sex: the capacity to desire and love an individual outside oneself and of a different sex characterizes adult sexuality. Now most perversions are the expression of fixations or regressions at one or another of the stages of the instinct's development, perpetuating, so to speak, a period of apprenticeship. It is what Freud expressed in the laconic formula: "One does not become perverse; one remains perverse." Any lasting sexual anomaly would be a fixation on some former hedonism, either a stopping point or a return to infantile or juvenile stages.

Corydon is indignant at the fact that a pederast could be con-

sidered "backward." [15] And, of course, he is not at all backward in
the physical and intellectual sense, but from the particular viewpoint of the maturation of instinct, he has indeed "remained" at a
stage of immaturity. With relation to solitary onanism, as an expression of integral narcissism and the total introversion of desire, and
from the viewpoint of the philosophy of instinct, some progress has
been made, since the libido directs its energies toward an object
outside itself; but that progress is incomplete and does not reach the
last stage, that at which the libido directs its energies toward an
object sexually different from itself. It is, as it were, an intermediary
stage between the desire of the onanist and the desire of the heterosexual, between narcissism and heterosexuality. This concept finds
confirmation in the basic narcissism of the huge majority of pederasts. "Proceeding as from narcissism, they seek their own image in
young people." [16]

In that perspective, the problem is to determine the influences
that hindered the maturation of the instinct and arrested its normal
development. But on this particular point, different schools have
different doctrines. Gide reproached psychoanalysts for their sense
of system. As he told me: "They want to apply their theory to
everyone, instead of reconsidering the dogma, or what they take to
be such, with relation to each individual case." [17] With no fixed
prejudice, I shall try to bring out everything in the first twenty-five
years of his life that can clarify his "individual case." Various com-
plex-creating situations, various psychic factors, moral and social,
encouraged a neurotic condition that was highly compromising for
the future of his virility.

"My puritanical upbringing made a monster of the demands of
the flesh." [18] A puritanical upbringing has often been blamed for
the sexual neuroses of a Rousseau, an Amiel, a Nietzsche, a Loti, a
Gide, to give only a few literary examples, and many psychological
novelists have treated the theme of the young Protestant who has
become sexually neurotic because of the severity of his confessional
mold. There is no doubt that the Calvinist regulation of habits is
particularly stern. As a Protestant philosopher, M. Arbousse-Bastide,
has emphasized: "In bourgeois society, the greatest sin is stealing;

[15] *Corydon,* p. 137.
[16] Freud, *Three Essays on the Theory of Sexuality.*
[17] "Dernières années," *Hommage à André Gide* (Paris, *N.R.F.,* 1951), p. 363.
[18] *Si le grain ne meurt,* 1, 247.

for a Puritan society, it is any sexual infringement." Yet the repressions and sexual deviations provoked by a too severely moral upbringing are less dependent on any one particular religion than on the personality of the educator and on that of the child he educates. The benefits or dangers of a rigorous upbringing depend, above all, on the one who gives it and the one who receives it. Both Gide, a Protestant child, and Rimbaud, a Catholic child, were brought up by narrow-minded mothers who saw religion as a constant constraint, and proved to be more concerned with having them live under the law than in the loftiness of grace. Even more rigid, intolerant, and domineering in that each had to react against a secret weakness, they increased the prohibitions and cast such a categorical interdict over sex that their anxious children imagined all the temptations of the flesh as coming from the devil.[19] Now by condemning sex as a "monster," a "dragon," a "demon," the Puritan ends by considering normal sexual satisfaction just as mortal a sin as any other kind of sexual satisfaction.[20] When in 1893 Gide made every effort to give his consent to the "demands" of his flesh, he added: "Even had those demands been more commonplace, I doubt whether I should have been any less perturbed." [21] That was characteristic of his puritanical turn of mind. The attitude of André Gide's family toward sex can be seen in all its rigor in a letter written to him by his uncle, Charles Gide, reproaching him for his relations with a "prostitute from Biskra," and going so far as to evoke the ghost of Lady Macbeth: "What's done cannot be undone." [22] Such intransigence, so foreign to Gallic humor, was not apt to encourage the young traveler in his attempt at "normalization."

What Freud said about Leonardo da Vinci's mother, namely that she had "stripped him of part of his virility," might be repeated, with more likelihood, about André Gide's mother.[23] Although her intentions were of the best, she seems to be that type of virile

---

[19] See above, bk. one, pt. i, chap. 12 [in the book from which this chapter is taken, hereafter referred to as *Delay*].

[20] I must also add that certain puritanical educators, Protestant or Catholic, would seem to have more indulgence for the onanism of adolescents than for any first normal sexual relations, as though in their eyes woman represented the sinner par excellence, as though Adam's sin, which lost him Paradise, had far more deadly consequences.

[21] *Si le grain ne meurt,* II, p. 287.

[22] January 20, 1895, unpublished.

[23] See above, bk. one, pt. i, chap. 3 [in Delay].

mother, so threatening to a son's virility, whom psychoanalysts do not hesitate to call "castrating." We know the role Freud gave to "that maternal divinity with the head of a vulture," and in most representations "endowed by the Egyptians with a phallus," in the evolution of certain homosexual cases. In the fable, Osiris—the child cut up into bits—managed to put all his pieces together with the exception of the male organ, and that legendary version has been used to represent symbolically the so-called castration complex. To go from there and claim that the threatening "crique" of Gide's childhood nightmares was merely a mother symbol is a big step and one an orthodox Freudian would not hesitate to take. But without turning to the elements of the psychology of the unconscious, particularly hypothetical in this case, we can find in Gide's history many proofs of his mother's inhibiting influence on his sexual development.

When at the time Gide was sent away from the Ecole Alsacienne and Mme. Gide learned that her nine-year-old son had "bad habits," she took him to a doctor who threatened to castrate him, but the prospect of such bodily punishment seemed not to have terrified the boy nearly as much as his mother's reproaches and the pain it caused her. He was fifteen when his mother warned him against streetwalkers in such a dramatic way that a few days later he had a fit of anguish, imagining one of his friends, a habitué of certain disreputable districts, as being "orgiastically torn to pieces by hetaerae." When he would read aloud to Mme. Gide, he was terrified by the idea of coming upon a "daring" passage, at which point his voice would "freeze," while his mother glared at him with an expression he described as either that of the captain of a ship, responsible for the fate of his fragile skiff during a tempest, or as that of an examining magistrate. When at the end of his adolescence he informed his mother of his plan to marry Madeleine Rondeaux, she categorically opposed it. He was so dependent upon her that his friends Louÿs and Régnier teased him about behaving like a "little boy." And he was already a twenty-two-year-old man when, in Biskra, Mme. Gide was so upset about his affair with Meriem that he agreed to break with the Oulad-Naïl and kept his word. Those are but a few of the more significant episodes.

"Each one," said Nietzsche, "forms his image of women from his mother; and according to the impression he keeps of his mother, he will esteem women or despise them, or be generally indifferent to them." That fairly questionable assertion would seem valid insofar as Gide is concerned: he formed a very special image of women from his mother, imagining them as paragons of virtue, respectable but not desirable, devoted to austere duties but unrelated to sensual pleasures. Yet ever since childhood he had embodied the opposite of such virtuous women in the image of his aunt, Mathilde Rondeaux, near whom he had felt "singularly uneasy," troubled both by "admiration and terror"; but the misconduct of Madeleine's mother caused her to be excluded from the family circle, and, anguished by the reprobation that weighed on the sinner, he had felt contaminated at the slightest contact with her.[24] Mme. Paul Gide's horror of sensual and frivolous women, and even more of "loose women," contributed to her son's "terror" of them.

In the evolution of homosexuality, psychoanalysts attribute major importance to the reactions of identification or rejection with regard to the parental images. Now among the very diverse family situations that have been invoked to explain disturbances in the normal development of the sexual instinct, that of Gide during his childhood is considered one of the most characteristic: the only child of an ill-sorted couple, with the father playing a very small part and the tyrannical and dreaded mother in authority. A homosexual is rarely the son of a happy couple, the image of complete conjugal understanding. And Gide was very young when his intuition told him that his parents were hiding a secret misunderstanding; furthermore, he persisted in trying to discover the flaw. On the other hand the obliteration of the father image, whether due to the father's absence, estrangement, or general discretion, is one of the traits psychoanalysts have often noticed in homosexuals. It was certainly part of Gide's condition, not only because he was only eleven when his father died, but because his intellectual, gentle, meditative, somewhat distant father, who dreaded domestic disputes, had given over to his domineering wife the task of bringing up their only son. "If my father had seen to my upbringing himself, my life would have been very different," André Gide told me when he was old, implying that he had lacked a father's presence; and indeed it would seem that the masculine influence in his development was insufficient in relation to the preponderant feminine influence. If it is true that in the case of many homosexuals one finds an abnormally close and prolonged dependency on the mother or on a maternal substitute, the dependency can exist in very different

---

[24] See above, pp. 142–46 [in Delay].

emotional types, going from enraptured love to more or less unconscious hate, and including all the ambivalent forms of love-hate. The love identification can be so intense that it leads to the desire for "dreaming, feeling, and loving like a woman," and even to the point of wanting to actualize "a woman's soul in a man's body"; but the mothers who inspire such abnormal, passionate feelings are usually very feminine, thus very different from Mme. Paul Gide. None of that applies to André Gide, whose dependency on his mother was doubtless close and prolonged but apprehensive and ambivalent, a mixture of the feelings of veneration and aggressive resentment, which contributed a great deal to making him a divided child.[25] Marcel Proust's love dependency on Mme. Adrien Proust, and André Gide's hostile dependency on Mme. Paul Gide no doubt contributed to making them both homosexuals, but different kinds, for one became effeminate and not the other.

"Our most serious vices are acquired in our most tender childhood," remarked Montaigne. Now as Gide himself specified in his *Journal* and even in *Ainsi soit-il*, his main vice was onanism, and actually his homosexual practices were merely substitutes for it. Although episodic masturbation is relatively commonplace, the same is not true when the habit becomes so inveterate that it defines the entire sexual behavior of a man as that of an onanist. This auto-erotic fixation can provoke other perversions, assuming that they are also the expression of narcissism, and it is in that way that the variously interpreted link between onanism and homosexuality has often been emphasized. "I didn't give up one of my two *vices* for the other. I mixed them together. Or rather, as each one took it upon itself to break all the obstacles of thought and feeling which might have stopped the other, it also seemed to provoke it," wrote Marcel Proust in *La Confession d'une jeune fille*.

When the organism is accustomed exclusively to solitary vice, as though it were a kind of "toxicomania," the sexual instincts become centered exclusively on the organ that gives the habitual pleasure, and desire cannot be transferred except to a human object endowed with the same advantage. Thus the very finality of the instinct—the complete union of the two opposite sexes—is thwarted; the homosexual is not attracted by the difference but by the homology that recalls his own sexual organ, the object of all his complacency. According to Freud:

[25] See above, pp. 124–25 [in Delay].

The high esteem in which homosexuals hold the male organ is what decides their fate. In their childhood they choose woman as the sexual object so long as they credit her with possessing that part of the body which to them is indispensable. Once they have acquired the firm belief that woman has disappointed them on that score, woman becomes unacceptable to them as a sexual object.

Very early in life, Gide imagined the female body as a multilated body which nature had considerably diminished by depriving it of a captivating organ. Moreover, when in his hallucinated daydreams Walter evoked the vision of "women's flesh," he at first found those visions tempting but in the end disappointing: "And I was afraid of seeing; I wanted to turn my eyes away, but in spite of myself, I looked. Under the dress there was nothing; it was dark, dark as a hole; I sobbed in despair." [26] He found the image not only distressing but terrifying; for the phantasm of sexual possession was linked in his youthful imagination to the fear of being "orgiastically torn to pieces." He dreaded the ailments suffered by those of Urien's companions who gave in to women, and dreaded even more the truly mutilating torture endured by Osiris or Orpheus. His was the same childish fear of mutilation through orgasm that psychoanalysis has discovered in the unconscious of certain homosexuals terrified by carnal possession.

In Gide's childhood and adolescence there is no trace of those ambiguous "friendships" which are often considered the starting point of homosexual habits. Yet apropos of his cousin Albert, twenty years his elder, he declared: "I vaguely suffered from his reserve, and I cannot help thinking today that he would have done me a better service by throwing it off." It is interesting to compare that laconic sentence from *Si le grain ne meurt* and a comment Gide made later in life: "If my cousin had initiated me, instead of letting me wear myself out all alone, I should have been an excellent family man." Here we have one of the strangest and most questionable ideas the writer of *Corydon* ever expressed. He deemed solitary habits so dangerous for any future virility that the sexual education of a young boy by an older man appeared to him advantageous and more normal. He actually believed that it would have made him "more virile" with women. All that is highly questionable, but there is no doubt that Gide's extraordinary and prolonged ignorance of sexual realities and his lack of any education in that realm did con-

[26] *Les Cahiers d'André Walter*, O.C., I, 170.

tribute to his deviation. He himself emphasized in *Si le grain ne meurt* the strangeness of his "themes of physical enjoyment," in order to bring out "to what point a child's instinct can go astray." [27]

Adler considered pederasty, in men of neurotic temperament, as the expression of an inferiority complex with regard to their virility; this interpretation is valid only in certain cases, but it is not unlikely in Gide's and seems to contain a measure of truth. According to Adler, the nervously weak man, who has doubts about himself and about his own virility dreads, above all, the deep humiliation implied in sexual failure, and seeks a way to assert, beyond question, his own superiority.[28]

Gide, still a virgin at the age of twenty-four, made, like Walter and Corydon, the sexual act into something terrifying, and feared that his "ridiculous ignorance" would make *him* ridiculous. Again and again, Corydon dwells on the difficulties an inexperienced young man has in approaching "the other sex" for the first time, and the ease offered by homosexual intercourse:

> Do you remember Daphnis' mistake and how he groped . . . And that is why, in Vergil, we see Damoetas still crying over Galatea's flight under the willows, while Menalcas was already taking his pleasure with Amyntas, and without reserve. . . . *At mihi sese offert ultro, meus ignis, Amyntas.*

His interpretation is specious, for desire is generally stimulated by difficulty, not thwarted by it; and the flight under the willows is merely flirtatiousness and should have provoked a chase, not, as with shy people, intimidation. Gide, whose Galatea obstinately fled from him for five years, and hardly out of flirtatiousness, was not obliged to make the slightest effort to get young Arabs, who offered themselves "without reserve," and the pleasure he took with them demanded no training whatever, for they merely revived his old habits. No inhibition intervened in his North African experiences with childish partners, especially as the differences in race and social class tended to neutralize the feeling of inferiority. Everything happened as if circumstances had helped him to follow his inclinations. His initiations took place in a country where pederasty is not particularly disapproved of.[29] The young boys he knew during his first

---

[27] *Si le grain ne meurt*, p. 62. See also, above, pp. 115–17 [in Delay].
[28] Adler, *The Neurotic Constitution* and *Inferiority Complex and Sexuality*.
[29] " 'Love is very difficult in our country,' Athman said, 'because the women are guarded by dogs and by the whole family' " (*Journal*, I, p. 87, n. 1).

two trips were accustomed to such practices and had no feeling of guilt about them. In the eyes of the little vagabonds who hung around the hotel, in Sousse as in Biskra, he was a rich and powerful lord, and all the more attractive in that he took part in their games with real amusement. He met just exactly the little sunburned boys Walter had dreamed of, and with them the puritanical convalescent, out of his element under that oriental sky, felt his austerity "melt away." Quite obviously, he tried to identify with the little foreigners, seeking an estrangement from himself which was also a return to the natural self he might have been before the puritanical and maternal ethics had intervened and at a time when sin did not exist. In fact, it seemed like a return to health. The blond, pure, wise, and dreaming child, contemplating some northern sea, whom he described in *Le Voyage d'Urien,* would doubtless have intimated Gide by his whiteness, his purity, his wisdom, and his dreams, for he would have awakened the guilt feeling in him; but Gide had no guilt when a little Arab "smilingly" offered himself in a strange country which left him no place for reflection. Of course, his desire was especially awakened by the bad little boys, but his tenderness went out to the others; and when he attached himself to one of them, Athman, for example, he at once began to moralize, wanting to bring him up—in the literal sense of the word. As he emphasized so many times, that tendency thwarted his sexual inclinations, as though the pedagogue inhibited the pederast. The "dissociation of pleasure and love" also regulated his homosexual habits; in him sensuality and sentimentality were opposed, but they are not opposed in *Corydon,* which is a theory of André Gide's habits not as they were but as he would have wished them to be.

There is no doubt that Gide's pedophilic experiences during his two trips in Algeria had considerable influence on the direction and determination of his sexual habits, and he himself confided to Denis de Rougemont that at that point he had made "a terrible mistake in taking the wrong road." [30] But was his attempt at "normalization" really compromised from that time on? His relations with Meriem had been satisfying. The fact that they were combined with a homosexual phantasm changes nothing essentially: if Gide had had a real "aversion" [31] to the female sex, as he subsequently

[30] Denis de Rougemont, "Un Complot de Protestants," *Hommage à André Gide* (*N.R.F.,* 1951), p. 283.
[31] *Si le grain ne meurt,* 1, 197.

declared, his first attempt would not have been brought to so successful and natural a conclusion.

Yet if that first experience was fully satisfying, why was it not followed up? Here, a series of adverse circumstances came into play and revived all the interdictions that had been cast over the female sex. First of all, Mme. Gide's despair, tears, and "inconsolable, infinite sadness" immediately transformed her recently emancipated son into the guilty child of old, and although he had the "cheek" to abide by his decision of seeing Meriem again, he did not, he said, have "the courage" to keep his word. As we know, his guilt feeling and anguish were such that his next attempt with the "much too beautiful" En Barka "failed miserably," and as he wrote to Albert Démarest, he felt that the harm done was "irreparable." Many months later he did get back some assurance in an Algiers brothel, perhaps because of the very "vulgarity" of the place and the girl, but the psychological benefit of his accomplishment was at once reduced to nothing by Pierre Louÿs' disastrous remarks on the girls' general state of hygiene. And so his heterosexual experiences were thwarted by anguishing feelings of guilt, inferiority, and insecurity, whereas none of those inhibitions intervened in his pedophilic relations.

If it is true that an unbroken chain linked the neurotic difficulties of childhood and adolescence to Gide's choice of homosexuality, his fate as a homosexual was not definitely established until he had made the choice itself. The actual moment he became aware of being, or thinking he was a pederast, and chose to assert himself as such, was at the end of January 1895, in Algiers. "I now found what was normal for me." That categorical awareness of his state, whether genuine or fallacious (there are homosexuals by conviction), had a decisive influence on the determination of his sexual habits, for self-awareness is a powerful agent of transformation, and man becomes, to a great extent, what he thinks he is. Was it the homosexual revelation in Algiers that led him to the highly assertive attitude so unusual in a doubter for whom every affirmation was a demand for asserting the contrary? The experience itself was probably less determinant than the circumstances under which it took place, the most important of which was the presence of Oscar Wilde. "There are people who would never have loved if they had not heard about love," wrote La Rochefoucauld, and that is even

truer about sexual habits which go against nature. There is, of
course, no reason to say that Gide would not have become a homosexual if he had not met Wilde, but it is likely that he would not
have so soon adopted, within himself, the attitude of the arrogant
pederast, determined to assert his anomaly as his norm. It was
directly after his meeting with Wilde in Algeria that he began to
think that what he had, until then, considered an inferiority could
represent, or be represented as, a superiority. His letters of January
and February, 1895, show the naïve, if not ingenuous, fascination
Wilde and Douglas held for him. The luxury with which the
aesthete and his Bosie surrounded themselves, their insolence, their
extravagance, their provocations, and their pretensions of being
patricians above the laws and morals of the plebs seemed, for a
time, to the son of the conventional and economical Mme. Gide,
to be the "higher immorality" toward which he had been aiming
but to which he had not yet dared aspire. There would be little
point in dwelling on such details were the pomp with which certain pederasts surround themselves not part of the prestige they
have with the very young. Oscar Wilde's vice, stripped of all the
glamor—the fame, the wit, the money—is no more than M. Mel-
moth's sad habit. It has been said that a vice cannot live without
mystery; actually, to certain people it is not viable without prestige.
Of course, a homosexual cannot have influence on anyone who has
not the same latent tendencies, but if it is true that such tendencies
are more or less latent in many adolescents whose tastes are not
conclusively established, an illustrious example can be partly responsible for numerous deviations. Gide was fascinated by the
"courage," or at any rate, the audacity, with which Wilde had
dared "be himself" and defy public opinion. The authority with
which the writer-actor had played the part of a homosexual character seemed to give Gide a kind of authorization to imitate him.

The minute a young man whose instinct has been repressed by
moral and social constraints decides to free sexuality from guilt,
he also generally rebels against the constraints themselves. Would
Gide's change in attitude have been very different if, instead of
deciding to free his "anomaly" from guilt, he had continued his
attempt at "normalization" despite his mother's prohibitions? It
would seem doubtful, given his essential puritanism, but the excep-
tional and censurable nature of the "originality" he asserted from
then on helped to intoxicate him with pride and strengthen his
protest. Determined to struggle for his sexual nonconformity, he

was led to extend his struggle to every other kind of conformity. As he later wrote to Ramon Fernandez:

> I think it's quite right to say (as you have done so well) that sexual nonconformity is the first key to my works; but I'm particularly grateful to you for already having indicated, after that monster of the flesh, the first sphinx on my way, and the most devouring of them, through what evolution and because of what invitation my mind, its appetite whetted, went even further and attacked all the other sphinxes of conformity, which henceforth it suspected of being the brothers and cousins of the first.

This passage would seem to show that those—and they are numerous—who consider Gide's attitude toward morality a consequence of his sexual anomaly are right. They base their theory on Charles Du Bos's diagnosis, namely that he was suffering from "generalized inversion," [32] and playing on those words, they see his sexual inversion as the point of departure for a general inversion of values. This thesis, which satisfies a widespread tendency to see a link of cause and effect between immorality and "immoralism," is simplifying to an extreme. Sexually abnormal people, outside of their anomaly, may go along either with the conformist's code of moral and social values or with the nonconformists': each one's reaction to his particular problem depends essentially on his own nature. The psychological motivations for Gide's immoralist protest were infinitely more complicated than the preceding thesis would give us to understand. What interests us at present is the fact that Gide considered his homosexual problem an integral part of his personality, for it thus took on major importance in his eyes. Just as Walter's psychology was constructed around Emmanuèle's love, so the "new being's" psychology was to be constructed around the justification of a vice. Needless to say, Gide was to find it all the more difficult to give up homosexuality in that he came to consider it the cornerstone of his personality, fallacious as that opinion may have been. His "virile protest," in the Adlerian sense of the words, was to be all the more uncompromising in that he came to consider his homosexuality as closely linked to his virility itself. Through a strange paradox, which was in fact not peculiar to him, giving up pederasty would have meant symbolic castration, because his assertion of homosexuality was so integral a part of his will to power.

It was one of Wilde's sophisms that largely contributed, if not to

[32] Charles Du Bos, *Le Dialogue avec André Gide.*

Gide's choice of homosexuality, at least to his rationalization of it:
the idea, so often put forward, of the aesthetic superiority of the
homosexual. Corydon not only claims that for a man to prefer the
body of an adolescent to that of a woman is a proof of taste, but he
asserts that "all periods of artistic efflorescence are accompanied by
an outburst of uranism," and he enlists a long procession of artists
behind Amyntas' crook, from Plato[33] to the present. There is no
doubt much of homosexual inspiration to be found in the works
of creative geniuses, as, for example, Freud remarked in Da Vinci,
Carpenter in Shakespeare, and Proust in Baudelaire, but it is impossible to conclude from that fact that they themselves were homosexuals. In the same way, the psychological makeup of many artists
shows an astonishing mixture of feminine and masculine traits, or
so-called from a Jungian perspective, yet there is no way of judging
their sexual behavior from that. It is true that uranism is far more
widespread in aesthetically inclined groups than in others, but the
fact is open to various interpretations. "I accept only one thing in
the world as not being natural: the world of art," said Corydon.
But once that axiom is stated, he refuses to use it as an argument
for his thesis, as Wilde did, for example,[34] for the good reason
that he means to prove that pederasty is "natural." We might
wonder with more probability whether the frequency of the link
between the homosexual condition and the aesthetic condition does
not come from the fact that both may be dependent, at least to a
certain extent, on the narcissistic condition, without claiming, of
course, as Schlegel did, that "every poet is a Narcissus." Some artists,
completely devoted to the creation of their works, dread passionate
love and procreation as though they were rivals: *aut liberi aut libri*.
Since neither Gide's heart nor his mind was involved in his homosexual relations, they had no lasting consequences and therefore
did not compromise his freedom. Moreover, the fact that homosexuality was then considered so reprehensible, especially by his
own Protestant and Victorian bourgeoisie, seemed to him part of
that necessary scandal—" 'Woe unto him through whom offenses
come,' yet 'offenses must come' "—which, according to the author
of *Le Traité du Narcisse,* had to be part of an artist's life. In his
unpublished journal of December 31, 1891, two weeks after his

[33] For a refutation of this point see Etienne Gilson, *L'Ecole des muses,* pp. 22–
23, 228.

[34] Gide's axiom, "vice is the father of all the arts," was directly inspired by
Wilde's remarks.

first meeting with Wilde, Gide wrote, and then crossed out, the revealing words: "The artist must know how to be something of a martyr." But such strategic intentions were to be brutally put to the test by the Wilde affair.

During the months of January, February, and March, 1895, the period that conclusively determined Gide's choice of homosexuality, he tried to justify his inclinations and worked out some of the arguments Corydon was later to develop with a far greater fund of information. But the first bit of rationalization or "crystallization" was suddenly compromised by the dramatic effect of the Oscar Wilde trial. A pervert cannot be intimidated, but candidates for perversion can very well be. Justice Wills's speech about Wilde's monstrous attempt at corrupting young people was addressed, beyond Oscar Wilde, to André Walter. Had the implacable verdict been pronounced in December, 1891, instead of four years later, Gide's fate as a homosexual might have been changed, for he was then still easily intimidated. He was far less so in 1895, but although he had foreseen the possibility of scandal and had consented to being "something of a martyr," he had never imagined that his attempt at sexual emancipation could lead to jail and hard labor. The last thing a free man wants is to be a convict. Noble as it may have seemed to defy the norms and judgment of society as Wilde did, "so certain of impunity," as soon as society avenged itself, he took fright at the atrocious punishment. And while the poet was on his way to Reading Gaol, Gide was shattered by another dramatic situation: his mother's death. In *Si le grain ne meurt* he affirmed that his mother had not even suspected his homosexual habits and had attributed his impassioned letters from Biskra and Algiers to an "affair," which she had begged him to break up. "The truth, had she known it, would have horrified her even more." [35] But was she really unaware of the truth? As she read about the details of the trial in the newspapers, had she not suddenly understood what was behind her son's strange attitude? She had read, reread, dated, annotated, and kept all the letters he wrote to her during the time he was seeing Wilde and Douglas, without quite understanding what they implied. Yet did she not suddenly understand, with deadly grief, the meaning of certain enigmatic phrases? Between Wilde's conviction on May 25 and the attack that paralyzed André Gide's mother at the end of May, the chronological

[35] *Si le grain ne meurt,* II, 361.

coincidence is indeed disturbing. Did he himself never think of it? As a child, and like many other religious and scrupulous children, he was inclined to make his "sin" responsible for any unfortunate events that may have occurred in his immediate surroundings; in *Les Faux-Monnayeurs* he described his alter ego, little Boris, as terrified by the idea that his vice made him responsible for the death of his father; and I have already pointed out the chronological link between Paul Gide's death and his son's fits of anguish.[36] Fifteen years later, upon the death of his mother, at the point when moral suffering causes childish terror in even the most reasonable of adults, did he not feed his guilt feeling on that kind of remorse? This hypothesis would more clearly explain the state of panic brought about by his bereavement, and the immediate and absolute need he had for "clinging" to his love for Madeleine, a pure Beatrice floating over the hells, the ideal image of a *vita nuova*. Such, in my opinion, were the circumstances that made Gide's prenuptial consultation a sincere undertaking.

Ruling out the possibility of a constitutional predisposition, and nothing would seem to indicate that there was one, Gide's homosexuality was not innate, and therefore fatal, but acquired, and therefore modifiable. It was not inscribed in his nature, but produced by diverse factors which had arrested the normal development of his sexual instinct, factors so entangled that to disentangle them would have been a difficult, but not impossible, task. He had a homosexuality neurosis—in other words, a sexual neurosis— which is susceptible of medical treatment, at least today. But in 1895 the methods of psychoanalysis were still in their infancy. Much later, when he was almost fifty, he discovered, and became interested in, the theories of Freud and especially of Stekel; he wondered whether he at one time could have been helped by such methods, and his reflections on the subject led to the episode of little Boris' psychoanalysis in *Les Faux-Monnayeurs*. But his inquiry was merely informative. Gide had long since decided that his sexual habits could not be changed; his sexual neurosis had become a perversion to which he gave his full consent and with which he shamelessly came to terms.

As for his physical aptitude for marriage, the doctor saw no problem because of the fact that he formerly had had normal

[36] See above, pp. 118–19 [in Delay].

sexual relations. Homosexuality, when not exclusive, is not, in itself, necessarily an obstacle to marriage. But the marriage of André Gide and Madeleine Rondeaux presented almost insurmountable difficulties, due not only to him but to her and to their whole relationship. What might still have been possible with another woman was not with her because of the inhibitions of both partners. Not only had Madeleine steadily refused him for five years, but she had clearly given André to understand that their union caused her "mortal terror," and even during their "difficult engagement" she had written to him: "I'm not afraid of death, but I'm afraid of marriage." And so Mme. Paul Gide's death had not miraculously removed the obstacles which were temporarily concealed by the exaltation of one and the compassion of the other. For reasons relatively independent of the homosexual problem, it was to be expected that André Gide's marriage, given the conditions under which it was contracted in October 1895, would be unconsummated.

The Role of the *Journal* in Gide's Work

by Alain Girard

. . . The Truth, what there is of it common to all of us, cannot be perceived *except* through the subjective, which at once conceals and reveals it. There *is* no truth except that of the individual instance. So it is the individual being we must scrutinize, in his most secret recesses, in order to discover (even in his dissimilarity to us) an aspect of that general law which explains him by setting him apart. Gide spent his whole life doing precisely this in his own case. Not for a moment did he examine himself with anything but a scientific curiosity—one of his earliest-revealed traits. This is the primary function of the journal in his life, and the reason for the place it holds in his work.

So important and so essential is the role of this journal that a whole book would be inadequate to describe it precisely and explicitly. I cannot pretend to do justice to the whole subject in a few minutes, so I will confine myself to suggesting, if possible, a few of the directions such an investigation might take, or rather to the determination of a few appropriate points of view. The proofs, the evidence for what I suggest would have to be found in innumerable quotations, in parallels and cross-references of every sort. Lacking such a critical apparatus, the insights I offer, despite their imprecise and tentative nature, may still open the way to a fruitful discussion.

Let us approach our investigation from the outside first.

All his life, Gide kept a *Journal*. Very early in his life, he allowed portions of it to appear in print. Later on, he published it himself, in its integral and definitive form.

"The Role of the *Journal* in Gide's Work" (original title: "Le Journal dans l'oeuvre de Gide"), by Alain Girard. From Marcel Arland and Jean Mouton, eds., *Entretiens sur André Gide* (Paris: Mouton & Co. n.v., 1967), pp. 198–215. Copyright © 1967 by Mouton & Co. n.v. Reprinted and abridged by permission of the author and the publishers. Translation by David Littlejohn.

The *Journal* extends over sixty years—from 1889 to 1949—which is to say, from his twentieth to his eightieth year.

To the approximately 1,700-page text of the Pléiade edition, it is proper to add several other books which fill in the gaps of that already imposing mass: *Le Voyage au Congo* and *Le Retour du Tchad* [*Voyage to the Congo*] of 1925–26, and later, *Les Carnets d'Egypte* [*The Egyptian Notebooks*] of 1939.

Two other books of Gide's old age have a right to be included as parts of the *Journal*: *Ainsi soit-il ou les Jeux sont faits* (*So Be It, or The Chips Are Down*), written "at random," wherever his pen led, and completed February 13, 1951, a week before his death; and *Et nunc manet in te*, reminiscences written by Gide after his wife's death, in which he includes several passages omitted from the 1939 edition of the *Journal*, in his concern to leave none of his unpublished writing to the discretion of posthumous editors.

On the other hand, the use of the *Journal* as a literary tool is systematic throughout his work, from *Les Cahiers d'André Walter* (in which, by his own account, he directly inserts portions of his own private journal) to *La Porte étroite* and the novel *Les Faux-Monnayeurs*—to select only a few of the more striking examples.

In *Les Faux-Monnayeurs*, the novelist himself assumes the stage, either because the narrative of events comes directly from his journal, or because he stops to reflect on the events that are taking place—or even on the very problems of the novel he is trying to write. He explains this himself.

> [. . .] I am keeping a notebook, from one day to the next, of the state of the novel in my mind; yes, a kind of journal, the sort one might keep of a child [. . .] Just think how interesting we should find such a notebook kept by a Dickens or a Balzac! Imagine our having the journal of *l'Education Sentimentale*, or *The Brothers Karamazov!* The history of the work itself, of its growth and development! Ah, but it would be captivating . . . more interesting than the work itself, I daresay . . ." (Second Part, chapter III).

Gide is perfectly aware of the excessive nature of this last affirmation; he is careful to put it in the mouth of his double, and express it conditionally. In the case of Flaubert, there would be a great deal to say, but one can hardly conceive of either Dickens, Balzac, or Dostoevsky keeping such a notebook. In them, the creative force is like a flow of lava, like a wave that nothing can halt—not even a reflection on its creation by the mind that is creating. They have their difficulties, to be sure, they have to fight their way; but it is an impulse far stronger than any critical spirit which permits them to exhaust the deep sources of their work. Like many of our contemporaries, Gide is fascinated by the "subcutaneous contact with the writer," as he remarked one day;[1] he loves to question himself concerning the problems of the work of art, and the intellectual or emotional mechanisms that make it possible. Moving from theory to act, he publishes along with his work *Le Journal des Faux-Monnayeurs*—dated reflections regarding his own novel-in-progress.

All of Gide's work stands as a psychological and moral commentary on artistic creation, and it pivots around the *Journal*. Without his journal, without the literary uses he made of it, his work, even the development of his thought, would be inconceivable.

Still, his *Journal* is not properly speaking a private diary, a *journal intime,* in the sense that the journals of Maine de Biran, Benjamin Constant, Amiel, or so many other nineteenth century writers are private—whatever hidden intentions these authors may have had concerning publication. Gide never deceived himself in this regard, and took care to call it nothing more than a "journal" when he published it. One could, further, instance many passages wherein he declares himself that the habit he had got into of publishing portions of it took away from his journal any character of "private confidant."

Does the publication of a text *ipso facto* take away its "intimate" nature? This is an important and a delicate question, but the consideration of it now would lead us too far astray. But the *Journal* of Gide lacks certain essential traits of a *journal intime.* To convince ourselves of this, all we need do is observe how it was composed.

Except during particular trips, which were to serve as the framework for a continuous narrative, the *Journal* is rarely maintained day by day. Most often, the interval between successive notations is one of several days. In all periods, one often comes across blank spaces of several weeks, a month, or several months, and a summary of the full and the empty days could not help but teach us something. The author himself is constantly warning us that the journal is a kind of self-imposed discipline, that he returns to it only when no other task is demanding his full attention, or even, on occasion, to set down certain ideas he can find no place for elsewhere.

[1] Jean Schlumberger, *Madeleine et André Gide* (Paris: Gallimard, 1956), p. 198.

He makes use of different notebooks, and distinguishes between the reflections he enters in one or the other. The notations which were to be collected into a small booklet under the title *Numquid et tu,* for example, had all been taken from a special green notebook.

A collation of the manuscripts (if they still exist), typescripts, and successive publications ought one day to be undertaken. It will be interesting to compare the variants, to which M. Rambaud has already drawn attention,[2] and which Gide himself made no effort to conceal. Let me pause a moment for one example.

It concerns certain passages, as Gide wrote, "dealing with Madeleine, which do not figure in the Pléiade edition." And, in a footnote, "Only the passages in italics appeared, occasionally somewhat modified, in my *Journal (1889–1939)*." There follow twenty lines dated September 15, 1916, in which one can, by comparing them with the earlier text, appreciate the nature of his modifications.

Gide has just torn out (after reading them to Madeleine) the last pages of a notebook which reflected "a dreadful crisis in which Madeleine was involved; or, more exactly, of which she was the object." Then he adds:

First Version:

And probably she was grateful to me for it [*m'en a-t-elle su gré*]; but yet I regret those pages; not so much because I think I have never written any like them, nor because they might have helped me to get out of an unhealthy state of which they were the sincere reflection, and into which I am only too inclined to fall again; but because that suppression made a sudden interruption in my journal and because, deprived of that support, I have since wallowed in a terrifying intellectual disorder. I have made useless efforts in the other notebook, I forsake it half-filled. In this one, at least [*au moins*], I shall no longer be aware of the torn pages.

Second version:

And probably she was grateful to me for it [*elle m'en sut gré*]; but *all the same, to speak frankly,* I regret the loss of those pages;

[2] Henri Rambaud, in *L'Envers du Journal de Gide* (Paris: Le Nouveau Portique, 1951).

not *only because I had never written any so pathetic,* nor because
they might have helped me to get out of an unhealthy state of which
they were the sincere reflection, *a state* into which I am only too
inclined to fall again; but *I also regret having torn them out* because
that suppression made a sudden interruption in my journal and because, deprived of that support, I have since wallowed in a *very
painful* intellectual disorder. I have made useless efforts in the other
notebook. I forsake it half-filled. In this one, at least [*du moins*],
I shall no longer be aware of the torn pages.

The changes are slight, but sufficient for us to catch the living
writer at work, recopying his own text and improving it in the
process. The first sentence was long, and he tries to lighten it by
cutting, without fear of a tautology; but he substitutes "any so
pathetic" for "any like them"—which produces a wholly different
sound; for "a terrifying intellectual disorder," which is flat, he
substitutes "a very painful" one, much stronger and more precise.
Finally, in the last sentence, by the replacement of *au moins* by
du moins he gets rid of a hiatus and adds a slight nuance of meaning.

This text may teach us something of Gide's method of operation
with regard to his journal, but it also introduces an important
question. We have in it the mention of a "terrible crisis," of which
we know neither the nature nor the causes. Gide's motives for
suppressing them are legitimate enough, since the text involves
another person. But may not the sentiments which Gide wishes
(despite this discretion) to have on record be altered somewhat
by the subsequent effort of writing them down? In reality, the
whole problem of expression could be thus stated—if not the
whole problem of art. To express an emotion—is that not already
to alter it? Then to refine or revise that expression—is that not to
alter it further? But if it is a question of rendering one's own
emotions, the only thing that counts is the exactness of the depiction,
and the effect produced, the echo aroused in the reader's consciousness. The question of "sincerity," so fundamental in the case of
Gide (a question to which we shall return) finds itself void of all
content from the very start.

On another occasion, much later on, in 1948, Gide warns the
reader that he is going to insert into his journal a few pages he has
just read over with disgust—but not without having done a little
"retouching" (II, 316).

A final, rather curious example. In the collected *Lettres de Charles
Du Bos et Reponses d'André Gide,* published in 1950, we find in-

serted at Gide's insistence "a page from his *Journal,* overlooked and not published by him." For the contents of this page, dated Pontigny 1928, I refer readers to this book.[3] But it seems odd to have "overlooked" such a page in the first place, odder still to have decided to correct that omission, almost on his deathbed, when the occasion presented itself in the midst of a quarrel in which he was passionately involved.

But if he has not perhaps seen fit to publish all he has preserved, Gide, on repeated and frequent occasions, chose to destroy rather than "retouch" many pages which he has not included in the *Journal.* On March 5, 1916, for example: "In the afternoon finished putting my papers in order, that is, classifying in series the pages of old notebooks that seem to me worth keeping, and tearing up all the rest. I tore and tore and tore, just as yesterday I had cut and pulled out the dead wood from the espaliers. How much there was!" And he adds a few lines further on: "I do not like anything in me but what I achieve at the expense of the most modest, most patient effort."

It is precisely the passages that were written straight off, then, like an outpouring of the heart, spontaneous and unreflected—the matter proper to a *journal intime,* in fact—that displease and embarrass Gide when he rereads them. At the very worst his journal, by reason of all these tearings-out, sins by omission. He has given a great deal of himself to his reader, but he has not given all. Or rather, he has given only an image of himself that is amputated, willed, and carefully put together. Not nakedly, not in his natural abundance, but shaped and controlled, stripped of all the branches that seem to him unworthy to bear fruit. But at the same time (to give him credit for a thing many reproach him with), an image aimed toward his highest conception of himself, in answer to the call of a "secret inner obligation."

So even were we not so informed by the author, we could hardly doubt that Gide's *Journal* is something dressed up, worked over, carefully arranged. There is a single entry for 1889, the first year of the published text, and it has the effect of an overture. It is the account of a visit he paid to Pierre Louÿs, in the attic-room of a house in the rue Monsieur-le-Prince, from which they could look down on the rooftops below. "At one's feet, just across his writing-

---

[3] Paris, Corrêa, pp. 11, 196–97.

desk, all Paris. To take refuge up there with the dream of your masterpiece, and not come out until it is finished. Rastignac's cry as he looks down on the City from the heights of Père Lachaise: 'And now . . . you've met your match!' " Private diaries do not begin like that. But that cry (which corresponds to Pierre Louÿs', "I need to *be* someone," in his journal for April 21, 1888) is the call of fame, and the hope that by sheer force of will the masterpiece that will bring him fame will come.

These few words were not to be published for many years; but when they were, they were selected from out of a great mass of *other* reflections, which Gide destroyed. Gide knew very early that what he was writing was not a *journal intime.*

> 8 October [1891]
> More than a month of blanks. Talking of myself bores me. [. . .]
> There is no longer any drama taking place inside me; there is nothing but a lot of ideas stirred up. There is no need to write myself down on paper.

> 3 June [1893]
> Useless to write one's journal every day, every year [. . .] The necessary simplification made them [my emotions] less sincere; it was already a literary restatement, something that a journal must not be.

> August [1893]
> . . . The desire to compose the pages of this journal deprives them of all worth, even that of sincerity. They do not really mean anything, never being well enough written to have a literary value. In short, all of them take for granted a future fame or celebrity that will confer an interest upon them. And that is utterly base. [. . .]
> I almost tore it all up; at least I suppressed many pages.

And, as a footnote to this passage, "Since then I have almost entirely burned the first journal (1902)"; the first seven years, 1889–95, add up to no more than fifty pages of the published journal.

What is more, Gide had not waited for his twentieth birthday, in 1889, to keep a journal. Here we must turn to M. Delay's indispensable work, *La Jeunesse d'André Gide.*[4] In point of fact, Gide began to keep a private diary from about his fifteenth year, just after he had finished his reading of Amiel's—a book that was then "all the rage," as he says in *Si le grain ne meurt.* "It would be absurd to pretend that without this encounter he would never

[4] Jean Delay, *La Jeunesse d'André Gide,* 2 vols. (Paris: Gallimard, 1956 and 1957).

have kept a journal," writes M. Delay, "for he was destined, as much by his complexion as by his complexes, to this genre of literature; even more, to what Paul Bourget (with regard to Amiel in particular) called 'the sickness of the *journal intime.*' But it is more than likely that his reading of the Narcissus of Geneva advanced his vocation by several years." Gide was not particularly anxious to acknowledge this influence, and approached this subject, as he did others, by a kind of hidden half-confession, since he does make mention of the reading of Amiel in his memoirs. But in his first book, overheated as it is by mere "literature," where a hundred of the most diverse authors are cited, "there is one name," notes M. Delay, "that we search for in vain [. . .]—a name, nevertheless, whose influence hovers behind so many lines—the name of Amiel"; and then he goes on "to render explicitly the line that connects the psychological state of a narcissist and that of the writer of private works."

The years when Gide reached adolescence were precisely the time when the posthumous journals of so many nineteenth century writers began to come out in force, when the reading public began to show an avid taste for these revelations, and when the fragments of Amiel's *Journal* won its author considerable fame from the moment they appeared. Without overemphasizing the subject here, it would be worthwhile for us to know just how far Gide accepted the journal-form as already established, at this stage of his life when the still-unformed self is so open and so susceptible to outside influences. It is not inconceivable that the young Gide, in his anxiety to *be* someone, made (quite unconsciously) something like the following calculation: as long as the great work of which he dreamed did not appear, he would always have his private journal to bear witness to the strength and originality he felt inside him, and to make clear his worth to others. But when the "great work" did come, later on, he destroyed this private journal, retaining from it only a few notes, perhaps improved a bit in their form, like so many benchmarks along the trajectory of his life, plotted from then on in a direct and definable line. Hence, in January, 1890:

> My pride is constantly being irritated by a thousand minute slights. I suffer absurdly from the fact that everybody does not already know what I hope some day to be, what I shall be; that people cannot foretell the work to come just from the look in my eyes.

Or again, on March 18, 1890: "Oh, those long days of struggling with the great work! The vision of them haunts me, and spoils me for all other work until I begin!"

There is no point in our wondering what Gide's real private diary might have been like; let us simply grant that it doubtless served him as a means of freeing himself, to a certain degree, from his complexes, and of allowing him to set himself at a certain distance from them—an indispensable condition for his work. But Gide was a man preoccupied more with himself than with anyone else, and one especially desirous of establishing in his own and others' eyes the image he was trying to make of himself. Years later, he was to write out memoirs of his childhood and adolescence, so as to absolve himself of the accusation of having kept things hidden, and as if to fill in the gaps left by the burned and torn-up journals. His entire life, from birth to death, was thereby to be laid bare to his own eyes as well as to others'. The ring would come full circle, the ring that enclosed both *Si le grain ne meurt* and *Ainsi soit-il;* the ring that had for its center the published journal, from which all else derived and to which all else returned—which is to say a reflection on man and the self at all points of its circumference. In writing his memoirs, moreover, Gide was obeying an innate and fundamental tendency of all *intimiste* writers, according to which the past exercises a dominant attraction, and in which the present— the time of the actual writing—is both a recollection of and an effort to reconstruct a past from which the individual tries to extract from himself an identity he feels escaping him. Although not really a *journal intime,* Gide's *Journal* (like the journals of other recent authors who have recourse to his mode of expression) still retains many of the features of the early "intimate journals," of which they represent only a new modality.

Gide's *Journal* is not, then, truly private; but it is, by another reckoning, something still more profound. What we find in it, essentially—in varying doses according to the period of his life— are descriptions of nature, travel-impressions, indications of his health, reading notes, a number of meetings with friends (and judgments concerning them), notes on literature and art, psychological or moral reflections, occasional references to social events, notations as to the progress of his books, and above all, the successive states of his thoughts and feelings on philosophic and religious problems.

No doubt this all represents a not insubstantial part of the most personal aspect of a man's life; but it still represents that part one is most willing to have others know. Of the truly *private* part, that which one ordinarily does not confide—of his amorous experiences, for example, which we know to have been so important for Gide— we search in vain for any trace in the *Journal,* except perhaps in the very last years, when the "life's work" is done, and when (more importantly) everything has already been thrown down before the public eye, when there is no longer anything essential left un-revealed.

What Gide had to say in this domain he certainly said—not in confidence to his journal, but in his other work. His sexual peculiarities were proclaimed in *Corydon,* at once a defense and an illustration of them, and in the second part of *Si le grain ne meurt.* His more subtle feelings in this regard are expressed in *Les Faux-Monnayeurs,* when Edouard speaks in the presence of Olivier. To express the most intimate aspect of himself, he needed the cloak, if not the mask, of art.

I do not know whether homosexuality is normal, as Gide pro-claims, but one may well wonder whether the discovery he made of the particular bent of his tastes did not serve his purposes so well that he welcomed it as a special sign. Normal or not, it made him different, and that was an appreciable advantage. We recall the little boy, crying in his mother's arms: "I am not like the others! I am not like the others!" Indeed he was not; and he must have suffered grievously from this feeling. But did he not, later on, construct his entire sense of self out of his pride in this very difference? . . .

Gide was as constricted and tied as any living being by his own private difficulties, and he kept writing all his life long in hopes of untangling the web and escaping from his torments. Above and beyond any judgment made on his work or his art, this would appear to be the central function of his observation of and by himself, through the agency of the journal.

Le drame gidien, the Gidean drama: according to several wit-nesses, Gide was made for happiness, not for suffering.[5] He did not *enjoy* his suffering; he always sought after a state of equilibrium.

---

[5] See especially Jean Schlumberger, *Madeleine et André Gide.*

It may well be that he reached it. At any rate, one may read the
Journal from that point of view:

> —as a journal of a *writer* first of all, who never stops reflect-
> ing on literature and art, and on his own personal efforts at
> creation;
> —and not as a *journal intime,* in which one goes back over
> his failings, his lapses, his weaknesses, in an ultimate and neces-
> sary effort to overcome them; but as a journal of his thoughts.

I make no pretension here of composing Gide's intellectual
biography, but it does seem to me that this long life has traced
a unique trajectory. A strange thing happened to Gide: many
of his nearest friends became converts, and he was very intimately
involved in a great wave of religious fever. But it was not a part
of his destiny to move in the direction of religious faith. Quite
the contrary: little by little, as if effortlessly, he won for himself
a kind of agnostic's serenity, by freeing himself from the constraints and inner divisions he had experienced for so long. It is
this very serenity for which some people most reproach him,
since it was achieved without God.

But did not Gide himself admit one day (November 6, 1927), "I
am an unbeliever. I shall never be impious." The supreme interrogation of a man in the presence of the world never ceased to strike a
deep chord in his being. After all, the answers each of us has to
make to this interrogation—what do they matter? What does matter
—and it is something by which the most hostile spirits can be
reconciled—is having heard the questions; having sought, without
respite or relaxation, to give proof, in the most personal ways, of
an effort in which one realizes the best in oneself.

Gide's *Journal* includes a good deal of dross, or rather it includes
a good deal that is insignificant in between pages of greater importance. It was not made to be read straight through, and I
daresay that very few people, outside of a few specialists, can
pretend to have read it all. A journal is not, by definition, a finished
work, and men who write or publish journals today would doubtless be well advised to remember this. For Gide, what it seems to
have been is a necessary means of creation.

What is it, then, that endures without qualification? It is still
and always possible to open Gide's *Journal* at random—to open,
that is to say, what of it he has allowed to remain and be published—

to skip over whatever bores or impedes, and to be certain of discovering here a purity of expression, there a piece of psychological insight. The works of a moralist are not meant to be read straight through either, and the value of the *Journal* of André Gide is to be measured by his own humanism and the wide culture to which it bears witness.

Chronology of Important Dates

1869   André Gide born in Paris, November 22, the only son of Paul Gide and Juliette Rondeaux.

1877–78 Attends (briefly) Ecole Alsacienne, Paris, followed by nine years of irregular education, in part occasioned by nervous instability and ill health.

1880   Death of Gide's father. He is subsequently brought up by his mother, on whom he remains emotionally dependent until her death in 1895.

1885   Period of religious fervor.

1887   Returns to Ecole Alsacienne; meeting with Pierre Louÿs. Discovery of Goethe and of his own literary vocation.

1889   Passes his baccalaureat.

1891   Introduced to the literary salons of Mallarmé and Herédia. First meetings with Valéry, Oscar Wilde. Publication of *Les Cahiers d'André Walter, Le Traité de Narcisse.*

1893   First trip to North Africa, with Paul-Albert Laurens: tuberculosis, convalescence, and first homosexual experience.

1895   Second trip to Algeria. Meeting with Oscar Wilde, acknowledgment of homosexuality. Death of Mme. Gide, May 31. Marriage of André Gide and his cousin, Madeleine Rondeaux, October 8. Wedding trip to Switzerland, Italy, and North Africa. *Paludes.*

1897   *Les Nourritures terrestres.*

1899   *La Promethée mal enchaîné, Philoctète, El Hadj.*

1901   *Le Roi Candaule.*

1902   *L'Immoraliste.*

1903   *Saul, Prétextes.*

1906   *Amyntas.*

1907   *Le Retour de l'Enfant prodigue.*

1909   Foundation of *La Nouvelle Revue Française* by Gide, Copeau, Schlumberger, and Ghéon. *La Porte étroite.*

1911   *Isabelle, Nouveaux Prétextes.*

1912   Serves as a member of the jury at the Rouen Assizes.

1913   Meeting with Roger Martin du Gard.

1914   Trip to Turkey. Works daily at the Foyer Franco-Belge (reception center for war refugees from the north) in Paris from November 1914 to May 1916. *Souvenirs de la Cour d'Assises, Les Caves du Vatican.* Break with Paul Claudel.

1916   Spiritual and moral crisis, writing of *Numquid et tu.*

1917–18   Beginning of liaison with Marc Allégret (b. 1900). In November 1918, Gide discovers that his wife has burned all of his letters to her soon after his departure for England with Marc in June of that year. Great subsequent depression, estrangement.

1919   *La Symphonie pastorale.*

1921   Gide's influence and enemies increase; attacks by Henri Béraud and Henri Massis.

1923   Birth of Catherine Gide, daughter of André Gide and Elisabeth Van Rysselberghe. *Dostoevsky.*

1924   *Corydon* (previously published in very limited private editions in 1911 and 1920).

1925–26   Trip to Congo (French Equatorial Africa) with Marc from July 1925 to May 1926.

1926   *Les Faux-Monnayeurs* and *Journal des Faux-Monnayeurs. Si le grain ne meurt* (previously published in very limited private editions in 1920 and 1921).

1921   *Voyage au Congo.*

1928   *André Gide* (volume of tributes) published by Editions Capitole.

1929   *L'Ecole des Femmes.*

1930   *Robert.*

1931   *Oedipe.* Growing interest in the experiments and the future of the Soviet Union.

1932–39   Publication of the *Oeuvres Complètes* in fifteen volumes.

1933–36   Serious political activity; anti-fascist speeches and articles, leftist offices and travels, climaxing with a disillusioning official visit to the U.S.S.R. in the summer of 1936.

1934   *Perséphone.*

1935   *Les Nouvelles Nourritures.*

1936   Trips to Russia and Africa. *Geneviève* and *Retour de l'U.R.S.S.*

1937   *Retouches à mon Retour de l'U.R.S.S.,* marking Gide's decisive break with the Soviet Union.

1938   Second trip to French West Africa. Death of Madeleine Gide, April 17.

1939   Travels to Greece and Egypt. *Journal 1889–1939.*

1940–45   Gide spends the war years first in the South of France, then (after March 1942) in Tunis and Algeria. In 1941 he resigns from the *Nouvelle Revue Française,* which is following a collaborationist policy.

1943   *Interviews imaginaires, Attendu que.*

1944   *Pages de Journal 1939–42.*

1945–46   Trip to Egypt and Lebanon of nine months.

1946   *Thesée.* Jean Dellanoy's movie version of *La Symphonie pastorale.*

1947   Awarded the Nobel Prize for Literature and an honorary Doctor of Letters degree from Oxford.

1949   *Feuillets d'automne* and *Anthologie de la poésie française.*

1950   Stage version of *Les Caves du Vatican* (written 1948) produced at the Comédie Française. *Journals 1942–49.*

1951   Death of André Gide, February 19. *Et nunc manet in te.*

1952   *Ainsi soit-il.* Gide's complete works placed on the Roman Catholic Index.

Notes on the Editor and Contributors

DAVID LITTLEJOHN, the editor of this volume, is the author of *Black on White: A Critical Survey of Writing by American Negroes* and *Interruptions,* a collection of critical essays. He has also edited the *André Gide Reader* and *Dr. Johnson: His Life in Letters.* He teaches at the University of California, Berkeley.

MAURICE BLANCHOT, the author of novels (*L'Arrêt de mort, Thomas l'obscur*), essays (*Faux-Pas, La part du feu*), and critical studies (*Lautréamont et Sade*), is one of the most profound of French literary critics and a radical student of the aesthetics of fiction.

GERMAINE BRÉE, Professor at the Institute for Research in the Humanities at the University of Wisconsin, is the author of books on Proust, Gide, and Camus (she is the editor of the *Camus* volume in this series), and co-author of *The Age of Fiction.*

JEAN DELAY, one of France's most honored psychologists, is the author of works on psychology, psychiatry, and education, as well as three novels and a monumental study of *La Jeunesse d'André Gide.* He is director of the Institut de Psychologie at the Sorbonne, and a member of the Académie Française.

ALAIN GIRARD is the author of *Le Journal intime* (1963), and a specialist on demography, immigration, and public opinion. He has been a Professor at the Sorbonne since 1964.

ALBERT J. GUERARD is Professor of English at Stanford University and a distinguished American novelist and critic. Among his novels are *Night Journey* and *Exiles*; his critical works include book-length studies of Bridges, Hardy, Conrad, and Gide. (He is the editor of the *Hardy* volume in this series.)

JEAN HYTIER is Professor Emeritus of Romance Languages at Columbia, where he taught for twenty years, and now Visiting Professor of French at the University of California, Davis. Of his early (1938) critical study of Gide, its subject wrote: "I think nothing better has been written on my work." He has edited the works of Pascal and Valéry.

LORING D. KNECHT, Professor of French and Chairman of the Department of Romance Languages at St. Olaf College in Northfield, Minnesota, is a specialist in the French novel and the teaching of French.

FRANÇOIS MAURIAC is the world-renowned French Catholic man of letters; has written more than a hundred books (*Thérèse Desqueyroux, Le Noeud de Vipères, Génétrix, Mémoires intérieures,* etc.). He is a Nobel laureate (1952), member of the Académie Française, playwright, journalist, and essayist; his "Bloc-Notes" have appeared weekly in *Figaro Littéraire* since 1961.

GAËTAN PICON is Directeur d'Etudes at the Ecole Pratique des Hautes Etudes at Paris and one of the leading French critics. Among his many books on contemporary French literature are studies of Malraux (under whom he worked in the French Ministry for Cultural Affairs), Balzac, Proust, and Bernanos, as well as the *Panorame de la nouvelle littérature française*.

JEAN-PAUL SARTRE, himself the subject of a collection in this series, is the world-famous philosopher, essayist, editor, playwright, and novelist, a leader of postwar European thought. He declined the Nobel Prize for Literature in 1964.

Selected Bibliography

The following bibliography, like this collection of essays itself, is intended to be no more than a practical *introduction* to the study of Gide. The student interested in further work will consult:

Naville, Arnold, *Bibliographie des écrits d'André Gide (1891–1952)* (Paris, 1952). The most complete bibliography of Gide's own writing (in French), although confined to book-length works. It will be superseded by the *Bibliographie chronologique des écrits d'André, Gide,* presently being prepared by Jacques Cotnam.

Martin, Claude, "Etat Present des études gidiennes (1951–1963)," *Critique* (July, 1964), pp. 598–625, and "Toujours vivant, toujours secret," *Etudes littéraires* (Québec, December, 1969), pp. 289–303. Scrupulous assessments of the current state of Gide scholarship, by the ruling master of the field.

Detailed bibliographies of critical works *on* Gide are scheduled for publication by Claude Martin (for studies in French) and Peter C. Hoy (for studies in English). Until they appear, the best source is:

Lafille, Pierre, *André Gide romancier* (Paris, 1954): Appendix, "Essai d'une bibliographie sur la vie et l'oeuvre d'André Gide (1890–1953)," when supplemented by the annual listings under "Gide" in the *French VII Bibliography* (New York) for 1949 to the present.

I. For the reader of English

WRITINGS BY GIDE

Afterthoughts on the U.S.S.R. (New York and London, 1938).

Autumn Leaves (New York, 1950).

The Correspondence between Paul Claudel and André Gide (New York and London, 1952; Beacon paperback).

The Correspondence of André Gide and Edmund Gosse (New York, 1959; London, 1960).

Corydon (New York, 1950, 1961; London, 1952; Noonday paperback).

The Counterfeiters (New York, 1927; London, 1927 [as *The Coiners*]; published together with *Journal of "The Counterfeiters,"* New York, 1951; also Modern Library, Penguin paperback. Latter published separately as *Logbook of "The Coiners,"* London, 1952).

Dostoevsky (London, 1925; New York, 1926, 1949, 1961; New Directions paperback, Penguin paperback).

The Fruits of the Earth, including *New Fruits of the Earth* (New York and London, 1949).

If It Die . . . (New York, 1935; London, 1950; Modern Library, Penguin paperback, Vintage paperback).

Imaginary Interviews (New York, 1944).

The Immoralist (New York, 1930, 1970; London, 1930; Vintage, Penguin, Bantam paperback).

The Journals of André Gide (1889–1949), including *Numquid et tu* (New York and London, 4 vols. 1947–51; abridged versions, Vintage paperback, 2 vols.; Penguin paperback).

Lafcadio's Adventures (New York, 1925, as *The Vatican Swindle*; under present title in 1928; London, 1925, as *The Vatican Cellars*; Vintage paperback, Penguin paperback).

The Living Thoughts of Montaigne (New York and London, 1939).

Madeleine (Et nunc manet in te) (New York, 1952; London, 1952, as *Et nunc manet in te*; Bantam paperback).

Marshlands and *Prometheus Misbound* (New York and London, 1953; latter title first published in English as *Prometheus Ill-Bound,* London, 1919).

Montaigne (New York and London, 1929).

My Theatre, including *Philoctetes, King Candaule, Saul, Bathsheba,* and *Persephone* (New York, 1952).

The Notebooks of André Walter (New York and London, 1968; first portion published as *The White Notebook,* New York, 1964; London, 1967; Citadel paperback).

Notes on Chopin (New York, 1949).

Pretexts (New York, 1959; London, 1960; Delta paperback).

Recollections of the Assize Court (London, 1941).

Return from the U.S.S.R. (New York and London, 1937; McGraw-Hill paperback).

Return of the Prodigal Son, in *French Stories,* ed. Wallace Fowlie (New York, 1960; Bantam paperback). First translated in *Yale Review* (June, 1929). With *Saul,* London, 1953.

The School for Wives, with *Robert* and *Genevieve* (New York, 1929, 1950; London, 1929).

So Be It (or The Chips are Down) (New York, 1959).

Strait Is the Gate (New York and London, 1924; Vintage paperback; Penguin paperback, with *The Vatican Cellars*).

Travels in the Congo (New York, 1929; London, 1930; University of California Press paperback).

Two Legends (Oedipus and *Theseus)* (New York, 1950; London, 1950, as *Oedipus and Theseus*; Vintage paperback. *Theseus* first published separately in *Horizon*, London, 1946, and at New York, 1949).

Two Symphonies (Isabelle and *The Pastoral Symphony)* (New York and London, 1931; Penguin paperback).

Urien's Voyage (New York and London, 1964; Citadel paperback).

SELECTED WORKS ON GIDE

Books

Brée, Germaine, *Gide* (New Brunswick, 1963). A new English version of a book originally published in French in 1953.

Guerard, Albert, *André Gide* (Cambridge, Mass., 1951, 1969; Dutton paperback).

Hytier, Jean, *André Gide* (New York, 1962, 1967; London, 1963). Translated from the French.

Three introductory surveys of Gide's life and works may also be noted, all sympathetic but all for various reasons inadequate:

Ireland, G. W., *Gide* (Edinburgh, London, and New York, 1963; Grove Press paperback).

O'Brien, Justin, *Portrait of André Gide* (New York and London, 1953; McGraw-Hill paperback).

Starkie, Enid, *André Gide* (Cambridge, 1953; New Haven, 1954; in *Three Studies in Modern French Literature*, Yale University Press paperback, New Haven, 1960).

Biographical Sources

Delay, Jean, *The Youth of André Gide* (Chicago, 1963). Translated from the French and abridged by June Guicharnaud.

Martin du Gard, Roger, *Recollections of André Gide* (New York, 1953; London, 1953, as *Notes on André Gide*). Translated from the French.

Mauriac, Claude, *Conversations with André Gide* (New York, 1965). Translated from the French.

Articles

Burke, Kenneth, "Thomas Mann and André Gide," in *Counter-Statement* (Los Altos, Calif., 1931, 1953).

Gosse, Edmund, "The Writings of M. André Gide," *The Contemporary Review* (September, 1909); reprinted in *The Living Age* (December 25, 1909).

Guerard, Albert, "*The Immoralist*: Turmoil and the Ordering of History," preface to Bantam edition of *The Immoralist* (New York, 1970).

Guggenheim, Michael, "Gide and Montaigne," *Yale French Studies* VII (1951).

Jackson, Elizabeth R., "The Evanescent World of The *Faux-Monnayeurs*," *Symposium* (Summer, 1962).

McLaren, James C., "Art and Moral Synthesis: Gide's Central Focus," *L'Esprit Createur* (Spring, 1961).

Parnell, Charles, "André Gide and his *Symphonie Pastorale*," *Yale French Studies* VII (1951).

Quennell, Peter, "André Gide," *Horizon* (June, 1942).

Russell, John, "The Old Age of André Gide," *Horizon* (November, 1947).

Sayre, Joel, "Lunch with Gide at the Dime Store," *The New Yorker* (May 22, 1948).

Sonnenfeld, A., "André Gide's Congo Journals: A Reappraisal," *L'Esprit Createur* (Spring, 1961).

Stock, Irvin, "A View of Les *Faux-Monnayeurs*," *Yale French Studies* VII (1951).

II. For the reader of French

WRITINGS BY GIDE

The fifteen-volume *Oeuvres complètes* (Paris, 1932–39), edited by Louis Martin-Chauffier, were not even *complètes* as of 1932, and are of course far from being so today. Nonetheless, they remain an essential tool for the scholar, being the only place in which many of Gide's shorter works are reprinted, and it is this text that is often cited in modern scholarly studies. An *Index détaillé* to this edition was prepared by Justin O'Brien and published at Asnières in 1954.

More useful, and more practical, for the general student are the three volumes of Gide's works in the series "Bibliothèque de la Pléiade" of Editions Gallimard:

I. *Journal 1889–1939* (Paris, 1939, 1940, 1941, 1948, 1951). Includes *Numquid et tu. . . .*

II. *Journal 1939–1949—Souvenirs* (Paris, 1954). Includes *Si le grain ne meurt*,[*] [1] *Souvenirs de la Cour d'Assises, Voyage au Congo, Le Retour du Tchad, Carnets d'Egypte, Feuillets d'automne, Et nunc manet in te,* and *Ainsi soit-il.*

[1] Works followed by an asterisk are also available in "*Livres de Poche.*"

III. *Romans, Recits et Soties, Oeuvres Lyriques* (Paris, 1958). Includes *Le Traité du Narcisse, La Tentative amoureuse, Paludes,** *Les Nourritures terrestres,** *Les Nouvelles Nourritures, Le Promethée mal enchainé, El Hadj, L'Immoraliste,** *Le Retour de l'Enfant prodigue, La Porte étroite,** *Isabelle,** *Les Caves du Vatican,** *La Symphonie pastorale,** *Les Faux-Monnayeurs,** *L'Ecole des femmes,** *Robert, Geneviève,* and *Thésée,* along with an introduction by Maurice Nadeau and invaluable notes (including textual variants) by Yvonne Davet and Jean-Jacques Thierry.

A fourth volume in the series, of *Oeuvres critiques,* to be edited by Claude Martin, is scheduled for publication in 1970.

André Gide was one of the great letter-writers of modern literature. His correspondences with many authors have been published, including the following: Christian Beck, Arnold Bennett, Paul Claudel, Joseph Conrad, Charles Du Bos, Edmund Gosse, Francis Jammes, Roger Martin du Gard, François Mauriac, Marcel Proust, Rainier-Maria Rilke, André Rouveyre, and Paul Valéry. The letters to and from Martin du Gard (Paris, 1968; 2 vols.) may be the greatest literary correspondence of the century. Of lesser, but still considerable, importance are those with Claudel (Paris, 1949), Valéry (Paris, 1955), Jammes (Paris, 1948), Beck (in *Mercure de France,* July and August, 1949), and Mauriac (in *La Table Ronde,* January, 1953). Others of comparable importance are now being prepared for publication.

Among the books not included in any of the categories above are:

Amyntas (Paris, 1906, 1926).

Les Cahiers et les poésies d'André Walter (Paris, 1891; re-edited 1930 and, less carefully, 1952).

Littérature engagée, ed. Yvonne Davet (Paris, 1950).

Corydon (Paris, 1924, 1929, 1948).

La Sequestrée de Poitiers (1930) and *L'Affaire Rédureau* (1930) have been reprinted, along with *Souvenirs de la Cour d'Assises,* under the general title of *Ne jugez pas* (Paris, 1969).

Théâtre (Saül,* *Le Roi Candaule, Oedipe, Persephone, Le Treizieme Arbre)* (Paris, 1942).

Théâtre Complet, 8 vols. (Neuchatel and Paris, 1947–49).

Anthologie de la poésie française (Paris, 1949).

SELECTED WORKS ON GIDE

Books

Albérès, R. M., *L'Odysée d'André Gide* (Paris, 1951).
Archambault, Paul, *Humanité d'André Gide* (Paris, 1946).

Arland, Marcel and Mouton, Jean, eds., *Entretiens sur André Gide* (Paris and The Hague, 1967). Valuable lectures and discussions.

Brée, Germaine, *André Gide, l'insaississable Protée* (Paris, 1953).

Davet, Yvonne, *Autour des Nourritures terrestres* (Paris, 1948). Sources and reception of the book.

Du Bos, Charles, *Le Dialogue avec André Gide* (Paris, 1946). By a Catholic friend turned critic. Important.

Fernandez, Ramon, *André Gide* (Paris, 1931). An early and still very readable study.

Hytier, Jean, *André Gide* (Paris, 1938, 1945).

Lafille, Pierre, *André Gide romancier* (Paris, 1954).

Lang, Renée, *Andre Gide et la pensée allemande* (Paris, 1949).

Massis, Henri, *D'André Gide à Marcel Proust* (Lyon, 1948). A doctrinaire attack by one of Gide's better-known antagonists.

Pierre-Quint, Léon, *André Gide, l'homme, sa vie, son oeuvre* (Paris, 1933, revised and enlarged 1952). The 1952 edition contains useful interviews with Gide and his former associates.

Biography and Memoirs

Delay, Jean, *La Jeunesse d'André Gide,* 2 vols. (Paris, 1956–57). Essential.

Herbart, Pierre, *A la recherche d'André Gide* (Paris, 1952). Intimate and unflattering.

Hommage à André Gide (Paris, 1951). Contributions of varying quality. *Note:* Drouin, Levesque, Camus, St.-John Perse, Martin du Gard, Mauriac, Delay, Schlumberger.

Mahias, Claude, *La Vie d'André Gide* (Paris, 1955). A photographic survey.

Martin, Claude, *André Gide par lui-meme* (Paris, 1963). Brief, but authoritative and well-illustrated.

Martin du Gard, Roger, *Notes sur André Gide, 1913–1951* (Paris, 1951). Drawn from his own *Journal.* Essential.

Mauriac, Claude, *Conversations avec André Gide* (Paris, 1951). Valuable testimony on the period around 1939.

Schlumberger, Jean, *Madeleine et André Gide* (Paris, 1956). A defense of Mme Gide against her husband's own recollections.

Articles and Essays

Alibert, F. P., "En marge d'André Gide," *N.R.F.* (January, 1930).

Bastide, Roger, "Thèmes gidiens," *Cahiers du Sud,* 328 (April, 1955), and 390–91 (October–December, 1966).

Boisdeffre, Pierre de, "Que reste-t-il d'André Gide?" *Revue des Deux Mondes* (February 15, 1961).

Desonay, F., "La conscience de l'écrivain chez André Gide," *Flambeau,* 5–6 (1951).

Ehrenburg, Ilya, "Le Chemin d'André Gide," in *Duhamel* [. . .] *vus par un écrivain d'U.R.S.S.* (Paris, 1934). A Russian assessment made before Gide's defection from communism.

Estève, C.-L., "Vers André Gide," in *Etudes philosophiques sur l'expression littéraire* (Paris, 1939).

Etiemble, [Réné,] "Le Style du *Thésée* d'André Gide," in *Hygiène des Lettres* I (Paris, 1952).

Ghéon, Henri, "André Gide," *Mercure de France* (May, 1897). One of the earliest intelligent appreciations.

Jammes, Francis, *"La Porte étroite,"* *L'Occident* (July, 1909). Of historical importance.

Jeanson, Francis, "Gide contre Gide," in *Lignes de depart* (Paris, 1963). A hostile view based on the Gide-Jammes letters.

Kanters, Robert, "Le Siècle d'André Gide," *Revue de Paris* (March, 1963).

Lévy, Jacques, "Psychanalyse des *Faux-Monnayeurs* d'André Gide," in *Journal et correspondence* (Grenoble, 1954). Ingenious if not wholly persuading.

Magny, C.-E., in *Histoire du roman français depuis 1918* (Paris, 1950), pp. 226–82. Contains an extensive and serious analysis of *Les Faux-Monnayeurs.*

Mann, Thomas, "Essai sur André Gide," *Echanges* (June, 1930). A translation of his review of the German edition of *Si le grain ne meurt.*

Picon, Gaëtan, review of "La Correspondence Gide-Valéry," *Mercure de France* (September 1, 1955).

Rambaud, Henri, foreword and afterward to Derais, F. and Rambaud, H., *L'envers du Journal de Gide* (Paris, 1947).

Rivière, Jacques, "André Gide (I: Style et Composition)," in *Etudes* (Paris, 1920, 1948).

Simon, Pierre-Henri, "Le christianisme d'André Gide," *Revue Générale Belge* (1951). One of several good essays on this subject.

Vallis, Geo, "André Gide, Son Journal 1889–1939," *Quo Vadis* (April–June, 1951). Intelligent.

Vikner, Carl, "Gide et Dostoevsky: Esquisse de la psychologie d'André Gide," *Orbis Litterarum* (Copenhagen, 1960), pp. 143–173. An excellent essay.

Weinberg, Kurt, "Gide romancier: La sincerité truquée," *Romanische Forschungen* (1956), pp. 274–87. One of the more temperate and intelligent of the "unfriendly" views.

TWENTIETH CENTURY VIEWS

European Authors

TWENTIETH CENTURY VIEWS

American Authors

TWENTIETH CENTURY VIEWS

British Authors

JANE AUSTEN, edited by Ian Watt (S-TC-26)
THE BEOWULF POET, edited by Donald K. Fry (S-TC-82)
BLAKE, edited by Northrop Frye (S-TC-58)
BYRON, edited by Paul West (S-TC-31)
COLERIDGE, edited by Kathleen Coburn (S-TC-70)
CONRAD, edited by Marvin Mudrick (S-TC-53)
DICKENS, edited by Martin Price (S-TC-72)
JOHN DONNE, edited by Helen Gardner (S-TC-19)
DRYDEN, edited by Bernard N. Schilling (S-TC-32)
GEORGE ELIOT, edited by George R. Creeger (S-TC-90)
T. S. ELIOT, edited by Hugh Kenner (S-TC-2)
FIELDING, edited by Ronald Paulson (S-TC-9)
FORSTER, edited by Malcolm Bradbury (S-TC-59)
HARDY, edited by Albert Guérard (S-TC-25)
HOPKINS, edited by Geoffrey H. Hartman (S-TC-57)
A. E. HOUSMAN, edited by Christopher Ricks (S-TC-83)
SAMUEL JOHNSON, edited by Donald J. Greene (S-TC-48)
BEN JONSON, edited by Jonas A. Barish (S-TC-22)
KEATS, edited by Walter Jackson Bate (S-TC-43)
D. H. LAWRENCE, edited by Mark Spilka (S-TC-24)
MARLOWE, edited by Clifford Leech (S-TC-44)
ANDREW MARVELL, edited by George deF. Lord (S-TC-81)
MILTON, edited by Louis L. Martz (S-TC-60)
MODERN BRITISH DRAMATISTS, edited by John Russell Brown (S-TC-74)
RESTORATION DRAMATISTS, edited by Earl Miner (S-TC-64)
SAMUEL RICHARDSON, edited by John Carroll (S-TC-85)
SHAKESPEARE: THE COMEDIES, edited by Kenneth Muir (S-TC-47)
SHAKESPEARE: THE HISTORIES, edited by Eugene M. Waith (S-TC-45)
SHAKESPEARE: THE TRAGEDIES, edited by Alfred Harbage (S-TC-40)
G. B. SHAW, edited by R. J. Kaufmann (S-TC-50)
SHELLEY, edited by George M. Ridenour (S-TC-49)
SPENSER, edited by Harry Berger, Jr. (S-TC-80)
LAURENCE STERNE, edited by John Traugott (S-TC-77)

(continued on next page)

(*continued from previous page*)